Mathematics Station Activities

for Common Core State Standards

Grade 8

WALCH EDUCATION®

MW01089574

1   2   3   4   5   6   7   8   9   10

ISBN 978-0-8251-6785-0

Copyright © 2011

J. Weston Walch, Publisher

Portland, ME 04103

www.walch.com

Printed in the United States of America

Table of Contents

Standards Correlations

The standards correlations below support the implementation of the Common Core Standards. This book includes station activity sets for the Common Core domains of The Number System; Expressions and Equations; Functions; Geometry; and Statistics and Probability. The following table provides a listing of the available station activities organized by Common Core standard.

The left column lists the standard codes. The first number of the code represents the grade level. The grade number is followed by the initials of the Common Core domain name, which is then followed by the standard number. The middle column of the table lists the title of the station activity set that corresponds to the standard(s), and the right column lists the page number where the station activity set can be found.

Standard	Set title	Page number
8.NS.1.	Radicals and Irrational Numbers	1
8.NS.1.	Rational and Irrational Numbers	9
8.NS.2.	Using Rational Approximations of Irrational Numbers	16
8.EE.1.	Problem Solving with Exponents and Scientific Notation	24
8.EE.2.	Rational and Irrational Numbers	9
8.EE.3.	Problem Solving with Exponents and Scientific Notation	24
8.EE.4.	Problem Solving with Exponents and Scientific Notation	24
8.EE.5.	Graphing Linear Equations/Solving Using Graphs	31
8.EE.5.	Writing Linear Equations	48
8.EE.8.	Solving 2-by-2 Systems by Graphing	56
8.EE.8.	Solving 2-by-2 Systems by Substitution	67
8.EE.8.	Solving 2-by-2 Systems by Elimination	77
8.F.1.	Slope and Slope-Intercept Form	114
8.F.3.	Relation vs. Function and Linear vs. Nonlinear	101
8.F.5.	Real-World Situation Graphs	88
8.G.1.	Transformations	124

(*continued*)

Standards Correlations

Standard	Set title	Page number
8.G.1.	Translations and Rotations	133
8.G.2.	Translations and Rotations	133
8.G.3.	Transformations	124
8.G.3.	Translations and Rotations	133
8.G.5.	Properties of Angle Pairs	140
8.G.5.	Properties of Lines Cut by Transversals	147
8.G.6.	Properties of Right Triangles	154
8.G.6.	Understanding the Pythagorean Theorem	161
8.G.7.	Understanding the Pythagorean Theorem	161
8.G.7.	Properties of Right Triangles	154
8.G.8.	Properties of Right Triangles	154
8.G.8.	Understanding the Pythagorean Theorem	161
8.G.9.	Volume of Cylinders, Cones, and Spheres	168
8.SP.1.	Data and Relationships	177
8.SP.1.	Scatter Plots	189
8.SP.2.	Scatter Plots	189
8.SP.2.	Data and Relationships	177
8.SP.4.	Data and Relationships	177
8.SP.4.	Scatter Plots	189

Introduction

This book includes a collection of station-based activities to provide students with opportunities to practice and apply the mathematical skills and concepts they are learning. It contains sets of activities for each of the five Grade 8 Common Core Mathematics strands: The Number System; Expressions and Equations; Functions; Geometry; and Statistics and Probability. You may use these activities in addition to direct instruction, or instead of direct instruction in areas where students understand the basic concepts but need practice. The Discussion Guide included with each set of activities provides an important opportunity to help students reflect on their experiences and synthesize their thinking. It also provides guidance for ongoing, informal assessment to inform instructional planning.

Implementation Guide

The following guidelines will help you prepare for and use the activity sets in this book.

Setting Up the Stations

Each activity set consists of four stations. Set up each station at a desk, or at several desks pushed together, with enough chairs for a small group of students. Place a card with the number of the station on the desk. Each station should also contain the materials specified in the teacher's notes, and a stack of student activity sheets (one copy per student). Place the required materials (as listed) at each station.

When a group of students arrives at a station, each student should take one of the activity sheets to record the group's work. Although students should work together to develop one set of answers for the entire group, each student should record the answers on his or her own activity sheet. This helps keep students engaged in the activity and gives each student a record of the activity for future reference.

Forming Groups of Students

All activity sets consist of four stations. You might divide the class into four groups by having students count off from 1 to 4. If you have a large class and want to have students working in small groups, you might set up two identical sets of stations, labeled A and B. In this way, the class can be divided into eight groups, with each group of students rotating through the "A" stations or "B" stations.

Introduction

Assigning Roles to Students

Students often work most productively in groups when each student has an assigned role. You may want to assign roles to students when they are assigned to groups and change the roles occasionally. Some possible roles are as follows:

- Reader—reads the steps of the activity aloud
- Facilitator—makes sure that each student in the group has a chance to speak and pose questions; also makes sure that each student agrees on each answer before it is written down
- Materials Manager—handles the materials at the station and makes sure the materials are put back in place at the end of the activity
- Timekeeper—tracks the group's progress to ensure that the activity is completed in the allotted time
- Spokesperson—speaks for the group during the debriefing session after the activities

Timing the Activities

The activities in this book are designed to take approximately 15 minutes per station. Therefore, you might plan on having groups change stations every 15 minutes, with a two-minute interval for moving from one station to the next. It is helpful to give students a "5-minute warning" before it is time to change stations.

Since the activity sets consist of four stations, the above time frame means that it will take about an hour and 10 minutes for groups to work through all stations. If this is followed by a 20-minute class discussion as described below, an entire activity set can be completed in about 90 minutes.

Guidelines for Students

Before starting the first activity set, you may want to review the following "ground rules" with students. You might also post the rules in the classroom.

- All students in a group should agree on each answer before it is written down. If there is a disagreement within the group, discuss it with one another.
- You can ask your teacher a question only if everyone in the group has the same question.
- If you finish early, work together to write problems of your own that are similar to the ones on the student activity sheet.
- Leave the station exactly as you found it. All materials should be in the same place and in the same condition as when you arrived.

Introduction

Debriefing the Activities

After each group has rotated through every station, bring students together for a brief class discussion. At this time, you might have the groups' spokespersons pose any questions they had about the activities. Before responding, ask if students in other groups encountered the same difficulty or if they have a response to the question. The class discussion is also a good time to reinforce the essential ideas of the activities. The questions that are provided in the teacher's notes for each activity set can serve as a guide to initiating this type of discussion.

You may want to collect the student activity sheets before beginning the class discussion. However, it can be beneficial to collect the sheets afterward so that students can refer to them during the discussion. This also gives students a chance to revisit and refine their work based on the debriefing session.

Materials List

Class Sets

- calculators
- rulers
- protractors

Station Sets

- 15 one-inch square tiles
- 18 small, equal-sized algebra square tiles
- 4 spherical objects of varying sizes (Ping-Pong balls, orange, basketball, globe, etc.)
- algebra tiles (10 blue, 10 yellow, 20 green, 40 red)
- colored pens or pencils
- geoboard and rubber bands for each group member
- measuring tape
- mini marshmallows
- paper towel roll
- scientific calculator
- scissors
- small square tiles or small square pieces of paper
- spaghetti noodles
- tape

Ongoing Use

- graph paper
- index cards (prepared according to specifications in teacher notes for many of the station activities)
- number cubes (numbered 1–6)
- pencils
- pennies
- scrap paper

The Number System

Set 1: Radicals and Irrational Numbers

Goal: To provide opportunities for students to develop concepts and skills related to simplifying radicals, performing operations with radicals, and classifying and comparing rational versus irrational numbers

Common Core Standards

The Number System

Know that there are numbers that are not rational, and approximate them by rational numbers.

8.NS.1. Know that numbers that are not rational are called irrational. Understand informally that every number has a decimal expansion; for rational numbers show that the decimal expansion repeats eventually, and convert a decimal expansion, which repeats eventually into a rational number.

Student Activities Overview and Answer Key

Station 1

Students are given 18 small, equal-sized algebra square tiles. Students work together to simplify radicals by factoring out a perfect square, using the algebra tiles as a visual reference. Students show two different ways to simplify a given radical by factoring out perfect squares.

Answers

1. $\sqrt{4}$; 4; $\sqrt{4 \bullet 2}$; $2\sqrt{2}$
2. $\sqrt{12}$; 4; $\sqrt{4 \bullet 3}$; $2\sqrt{3}$
3. $\sqrt{18}$; 9; $\sqrt{9 \bullet 2}$; $3\sqrt{2}$
4. $\sqrt{48} = \sqrt{16 \bullet 3} = 4\sqrt{3}$ and $\sqrt{48} = \sqrt{12 \bullet 4} = 2\sqrt{12} = 2\sqrt{4 \bullet 3} = 4\sqrt{3}$

Station 2

Students are given 12 index cards with the following numbers written on them:

$$-25\sqrt{12}, 3\sqrt{12}, -8\sqrt{3}, \sqrt{3}, 10\sqrt{7}, 12\sqrt{10}, -4\sqrt{10}, 100\sqrt{10},$$
$$12\sqrt{15}, -20\sqrt{15}, 15\sqrt{21}, 21\sqrt{21}$$

The index cards will be shuffled. One student will deal each student an equal number of cards (i.e., if there are four students, then each student will receive three cards). Each student will place one of their cards in the center of the table. Students will work together to determine which radicals can be added together or subtracted.

Answers

1. Answers will vary. Possible answers:
$$-25\sqrt{12} + 3\sqrt{12} = -22\sqrt{12} \text{ and } -25\sqrt{12} - 3\sqrt{12} = -28\sqrt{12} \text{ OR}$$
$$3\sqrt{12} - (-25\sqrt{12}) = 28\sqrt{12}$$

2. Answers will vary. Possible answers:
$$12\sqrt{10} + 100\sqrt{10} = 112\sqrt{10} \text{ and } 12\sqrt{10} - 100\sqrt{10} = -88\sqrt{10} \text{ OR}$$
$$100\sqrt{10} - 12\sqrt{10} = 88\sqrt{10}$$

3. Answers will vary. Possible answers:
$$15\sqrt{21} + 21\sqrt{21} = 36\sqrt{21} \text{ and } 15\sqrt{21} - 21\sqrt{21} = -6\sqrt{21} \text{ OR}$$
$$21\sqrt{21} - 6\sqrt{21} = 15\sqrt{21}$$

4. The radicands have to be equal.

Station 3

Students are given 12 index cards with the following numbers written on them:

$$5\sqrt{12},\ 3\sqrt{4}, -8\sqrt{15},\ 6\sqrt{6},\ 12\sqrt{10}, -4\sqrt{10},\ 7\sqrt{2},\ 8\sqrt{20},\ 12\sqrt{10},\ 15\sqrt{20},\ 3\sqrt{5},\ \sqrt{30}$$

Students will draw two cards at a time from the pile of index cards. They will work together to multiply and divide the radicals on the index cards and record their answers in a table.

Answers

Answers will vary. Possible answers:

Index card #1	Index card #2	Multiplication	Division
$5\sqrt{12}$	$3\sqrt{4}$	$15\sqrt{48} = 60\sqrt{3}$	$\dfrac{5\sqrt{12}}{3\sqrt{4}} = \dfrac{5\sqrt{3}}{3}$
$6\sqrt{6}$	$-4\sqrt{10}$	$-24\sqrt{60} = -48\sqrt{15}$	$\dfrac{6\sqrt{6}}{-4\sqrt{10}} = \dfrac{3\sqrt{3}}{-2\sqrt{5}}$

Station 4

Students use two number cubes to generate two numbers. They work together to arrange the two numbers as a rational number and an irrational number. Students give their reasoning behind creating rational and irrational numbers for the same two numbers.

Answers

1–4. Answers will vary.

Materials List/Setup

Station 1	18 small, equal-sized algebra square tiles
Station 2	12 index cards with the following numbers written on them:

$$-25\sqrt{12},\; 3\sqrt{12},\; -8\sqrt{3},\; \sqrt{3},\; 10\sqrt{7},\; 12\sqrt{10},\; -4\sqrt{10},$$
$$100\sqrt{10},\; 12\sqrt{15},\; -20\sqrt{15},\; 15\sqrt{21},\; 21\sqrt{21}$$

Station 3	12 index cards with the following numbers written on them:

$$5\sqrt{12},\; 3\sqrt{4},\; -8\sqrt{15},\; 6\sqrt{6},\; 12\sqrt{10},\; -4\sqrt{10},$$
$$7\sqrt{2},\; 8\sqrt{20},\; 12\sqrt{10},\; 15\sqrt{20},\; 3\sqrt{5},\; \sqrt{30}$$

Station 4	two number cubes

Discussion Guide

To support students in reflecting on the activities and to gather formative information about student learning, use the following prompts to facilitate a class discussion to "debrief" the station activities.

Prompts/Questions

1. How do you simplify radicals using a perfect square?

2. Provide three real-world examples of when you would use and simplify radicals.

3. What has to be equal in order to add and subtract radical numbers? What is this quantity called?

4. How do you add and subtract radical numbers?

5. How do you multiply and divide radical numbers?

6. How can you tell if a number is rational or irrational?

Think, Pair, Share

Have students jot down their own responses to questions, then discuss with a partner (who was not in their station group), and then discuss as a whole class.

Suggested Appropriate Responses

1. Factor out the perfect square and then take the square root of each number.

2. Answers may vary. Possible answers: Construction—using the Pythagorean theorem to construct triangular woodwork; Physics—using radicals in distance and acceleration equations; Finance—using radicals in calculations such as net present value.

3. The quantity under the radical sign is known as the radicand.

4. Add and/or subtract the numbers in front of the radical. Leave the radicand the same.

5. For multiplication, multiply the numbers in front of the radical. Multiply the radicands. For division, divide the numbers in front of the radical. Divide the radicands.

6. A rational number can be expressed exactly by a ratio of two integers. An irrational number cannot be expressed exactly by a ratio of two integers.

Possible Misunderstandings/Mistakes

- When a perfect square is identified, not taking the square root of the number before placing it in front of the radical

- Adding or subtracting radicals that do not have the same radicand

- Adding or subtracting the radicands

- Not multiplying or dividing the radicands in addition to multiplying and dividing the numbers in front of the radical

The Number System
Set 1: Radicals and Irrational Numbers

Station 1

You will be given 18 square algebra tiles and will need to simplify $\sqrt{8}$, $\sqrt{12}$, and $\sqrt{18}$. Work together to create a group of 8 algebra tiles, factor out a perfect square, and simplify the radical. Repeat this process for a group of 12 algebra tiles and then 18 algebra tiles. Write your answers below.

1. Simplify $\sqrt{8}$.

    What perfect square can you factor out of $\sqrt{8}$? _____

    Rewrite the original radical in factored form: _____

    Find the square root of the perfect square and write your final answer for $\sqrt{8}$.

2. Simplify $\sqrt{12}$.

    What perfect square can you factor out of $\sqrt{12}$? _____

    Rewrite the original radical in factored form: _____

    Find the square root of the perfect square and write your final answer for $\sqrt{12}$.

3. Simplify $\sqrt{18}$.

    What perfect square can you factor out of $\sqrt{18}$? _____

    Rewrite the original radical in factored form: _____

    Find the square root of the perfect square and write your final answer for $\sqrt{18}$.

4. In the space below, show two different ways to simplify $\sqrt{48}$ by factoring out perfect squares.

The Number System
Set 1: Radicals and Irrational Numbers

Station 2

You will be given 12 index cards with the following numbers written on them:

$$-25\sqrt{12}, \; 3\sqrt{12}, \; -8\sqrt{3}, \; \sqrt{3}, \; 10\sqrt{7}, \; 12\sqrt{10}, \; -4\sqrt{10},$$

$$100\sqrt{10}, \; 12\sqrt{15}, \; -20\sqrt{15}, \; 15\sqrt{21}, \; 21\sqrt{21}$$

Shuffle the index cards. Have one group member deal each of you an equal number of cards (i.e., if there are four students, then each one will receive three cards). Have each student place one of their cards in the center of the table. Work together to determine which radicals can be added together or subtracted. If none of the radicals can be added or subtracted, then place a round of new cards on the table. Repeat this process with your remaining cards. If time permits, reshuffle the cards and play again.

1. What radicals could be added and subtracted in round one? _____

    Add and subtract these radicals: _____

2. What radicals could be added and subtracted in round two? _____

    Add and subtract these radicals: _____

3. What radicals could be added and subtracted in round three? _____

    Add and subtract these radicals: _____

4. How did you know which radicals could be added or subtracted?

The Number System
Set 1: Radicals and Irrational Numbers

Station 3

You will be given 12 index cards with the following numbers written on them:

$$5\sqrt{12},\ 3\sqrt{4},\ -8\sqrt{15},\ 6\sqrt{6},\ 12\sqrt{10},\ -4\sqrt{10},\ 7\sqrt{2},\ 8\sqrt{20},\ 12\sqrt{10},\ 15\sqrt{20},\ 3\sqrt{5},\ \sqrt{30}$$

Place the index cards in a pile. Have one student draw two index cards. Work together to multiply and divide the radicals on the index cards. Repeat this process with your remaining cards. If time permits, reshuffle the cards and play again.

Record the index cards and your answers in the table below. Remember to simplify your answer.

Index card #1	Index card #2	Multiplication	Division

The Number System
Set 1: Radicals and Irrational Numbers

Station 4

Use the two number cubes provided for problems 1–4.

1. Roll each number cube and record the results in the boxes below.

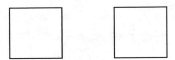

2. Work with other students to arrange these two numbers so they make up a rational number. Write your answer below. Give a reason for your answer.

3. Work with other students to arrange these two numbers so that they are irrational. Write your answer below. Give a reason for your answer.

4. Repeat the process three more times.

The Number System

Set 2: Rational and Irrational Numbers

Goal: To provide opportunities for students to develop concepts and skills related to rational and irrational numbers

Common Core Standards

The Number System

Know that there are numbers that are not rational, and approximate them by rational numbers.

8.NS.1. Know that numbers that are not rational are called irrational. Understand informally that every number has a decimal expansion; for rational numbers show that the decimal expansion repeats eventually, and convert a decimal expansion, which repeats eventually into a rational number.

Expressions and Equations

Work with radicals and integer exponents.

8.EE.2. Use square root and cube root symbols to represent solutions to equations of the form $x^2 = p$ and $x^3 = p$, where p is a positive rational number. Evaluate square roots of small perfect squares and cube roots of small perfect cubes. Know that $\sqrt{2}$ is irrational.

Student Activities Overview and Answer Key

Station 1

Students use a calculator to write decimal expansions for several given numbers. They work together to identify repeating decimals and terminating decimals (rational numbers), and they make a conjecture about the numbers whose decimal expansions are neither repeating nor terminating (these numbers are irrational).

Answers: 1. 0.875; 2. $0.\overline{2}$; 3. $4.1\overline{6}$; 4. 14; 5. 4.1231056; 6. 3.1415926; 7. 15.625; 8. $0.08\overline{3}$

Terminating decimals: $7/8$, $\sqrt{196}$, $(2.5)^3$

Repeating decimals: $2/9$, $4\,1/6$, $1/12$

Neither: $\sqrt{17}$, π (these numbers are irrational)

Station 2

Students use a number cube to create radicals with two-digit radicands. Students work together to decide if each radical is a rational number or an irrational number. Students write reasons for their responses.

Answers: Answers will vary depending upon the numbers rolled.

Possible reasons: If the radicand is a perfect square, the number is rational. Otherwise it is irrational.

Station 3

Students are given a set of ten cards with numbers on them. The goal is to sort the cards into two piles. One pile should contain only rational numbers, and the other should contain only irrational numbers. Once students have sorted the cards, they reflect on the strategies they used.

Answers: Rational: $3/5$, $0.\overline{8}$, $\sqrt{4}$, $\sqrt{16}$, -2, 0, 4.173
Irrational: $\sqrt{2}$, $\sqrt{5}$, π

Possible strategies: Begin by looking for whole numbers, fractions, and repeating or terminating decimals. These are all rational. For radicals, determine whether the radicand is a perfect square. If so, the number is rational. If not, the number is irrational.

Station 4

Students are given a set of eight cards with numbers on them. They use the cards to form four radicals with two-digit radicands. The goal is to create two rational numbers and two irrational numbers. Once they have formed the radicals, students work together to check their work and reflect on their strategies.

Answers: There are several correct ways to form the radicals. One possibility is $\sqrt{16}$ and $\sqrt{25}$ (rational), and $\sqrt{41}$ and $\sqrt{96}$ (irrational).

Possible strategies: Begin by using pairs of cards to form two-digit perfect squares. The square roots of these numbers are rational. Use the leftover cards to form two-digit numbers that are not perfect squares. The square roots of these numbers are irrational.

Materials List/Setup

Station 1   calculator

Station 2   number cube (numbered 1–6)

Station 3   10 index cards with the following numbers written on them:
$3/5$, 0.8, $\sqrt{4}$, $\sqrt{16}$, -2, 0, 4.173, $\sqrt{2}$, $\sqrt{5}$, π

Station 4   8 index cards with the following numbers written on them:
1, 1, 2, 4, 5, 6, 6, 9

Discussion Guide

To support students in reflecting on the activities and to gather some formative information about student learning, use the following prompts to facilitate a class discussion to "debrief" the station activities.

Prompts/Questions

1. What does it mean for a number to be rational?

2. Is every whole number rational? Why or why not?

3. What can you say about the decimal expansion of a rational number?

4. How can you use a calculator to help you decide if a number is rational?

Think, Pair, Share

Have students jot down their own responses to questions, then discuss with a partner (who was not in their station group), and then discuss as a whole class.

Suggested Appropriate Responses

1. The number can be written as a fraction (i.e., as a quotient of two whole numbers). Equivalently, the number is a terminating or repeating decimal.

2. Yes. It may be written as a fraction with a denominator of 1.

3. It is either repeating or terminating.

4. Use the calculator to convert the number to a decimal. If the decimal is repeating or terminating, the number is rational.

Possible Misunderstandings/Mistakes

- Assuming that any square root is irrational
- Not realizing that any number written as a fraction must be rational
- Incorrectly simplifying radicals
- Incorrectly converting between fractions and decimals

The Number System
Set 2: Rational and Irrational Numbers

Station 1

You will need a calculator for this activity.

Use the calculator to help you write each of the following numbers as a decimal. Work together to decide how to use the calculator to convert the numbers to decimals.

1. $\dfrac{7}{8}$

2. $\dfrac{2}{9}$

3. $4\dfrac{1}{6}$

4. $\sqrt{196}$

5. $\sqrt{17}$

6. π

7. $(2.5)^3$

8. $\dfrac{1}{12}$

Work together to identify the numbers that have terminating decimals. Write them below.

_____

Work together to identify the numbers that have repeating decimals. Write them below.

_____

Write the numbers that do not appear to have terminating or repeating decimals.

_____

What can you say about the numbers that don't have terminating or repeating decimals?

_____

_____

The Number System
Set 2: Rational and Irrational Numbers

Station 2

You will find a number cube at this station. Use the number cube to create square roots.

Roll the number cube two times. Write the two numbers in the boxes inside the radical sign below.

Work with other students to decide if the radical is a rational number or an irrational number. Write your answer below. Give a reason for your answer.

_____

_____

Repeat the process four more times.

          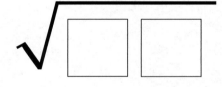

_____   _____

_____   _____

_____   _____

_____   _____

          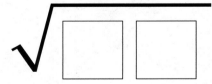

_____   _____

_____   _____

_____   _____

_____   _____

The Number System
Set 2: Rational and Irrational Numbers

Station 3

You will find a set of 10 cards at this station. The cards have the following numbers written on them:

$$0 \qquad \frac{3}{5} \qquad \sqrt{2} \qquad 0.\overline{8} \qquad \pi \qquad \sqrt{4} \qquad \sqrt{16} \qquad -2 \qquad \sqrt{5} \qquad 4.173$$

Work with other students to sort the cards into two piles. One pile should contain only rational numbers. The other pile should contain only irrational numbers.

Write your results below.

Rational: _____

Irrational: _____

Work together to check that you have sorted the numbers correctly. Describe any strategies you could use to solve this problem.

_____

_____

_____

The Number System
Set 2: Rational and Irrational Numbers

Station 4

You will be given a set of eight index cards. The cards have the following numbers written on them:

1	1	2	4	5	6	6	9

Write numbers in the boxes to form four radicals of two-digit numbers. The goal is to create two rational numbers and two irrational numbers.

 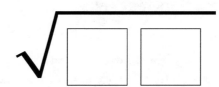

Work together to check that you have created two rational numbers and two irrational numbers. Write the numbers below.

Rational: _____

Irrational: _____

Explain the strategies you could use to solve this problem.

_____

_____

_____

The Number System

Goal: To provide students with opportunities to use rational approximations of irrational numbers for a variety of purposes

Common Core Standards

The Number System

Know that there are numbers that are not rational, and approximate them by rational numbers.

8.NS.2. Use rational approximations of irrational numbers to compare the size of irrational numbers, locate them approximately on a number line diagram, and estimate the value of expressions (e.g., π^2).

Student Activities Overview and Answer Key

Station 1

Students will use a rational approximation of π to compare it to the rational number 3.20. Importantly, they will explain how to approximate π and how to evaluate greater than or less than in comparison with a rational number.

Answers

1. 3.14159265358979323846264433832795...

2. 3.14

3. less than

4. Alicia will want to be paid \$3.20 per hour because this way she will earn more money than if she were paid \$$\pi$ per hour. The number π can be approximated or rounded to 3.14, which is less than 3.20.

5. π is irrational because it is a decimal that does not terminate or repeat; it can't be expressed as a fraction.

6. Answers will vary, but should include the idea that the irrational number needs to be rounded or truncated to one decimal place beyond the rational number to which it is being compared.

Station 2

Students will roll a number cube and compare the number they rolled to the square root of the number they rolled. They will approximate the square root of the number when necessary and place it on the number line.

Answers

1–4. Answers will vary depending on the number rolled. Answers for each possible roll, rounded to the nearest hundredth:

Number rolled	Square root	Value of square root
1	$\sqrt{1}$	1
2	$\sqrt{2}$	1.41
3	$\sqrt{3}$	1.73
4	$\sqrt{4}$	2
5	$\sqrt{5}$	2.24
6	$\sqrt{6}$	2.45

5. Sample answer: Round the irrational number to the hundredths place to approximate where it should be placed on the number line.

Station 3

Students will approximate the value of $\sqrt{2}$ in order to estimate the value of the expression $3\sqrt{2}$. They will explain how they approximated and why they needed to use a rational number to estimate the value of the expression.

Answers

1. 1.4142135623730950

2. 1.4

3. $3\sqrt{2}$ inches

4. 4.2 inches

5. 4.2 inches or about 4¼ inches on a ruler

6. Answers will vary, but should include the fact that an irrational number doesn't have a terminating or repeating decimal and it's impossible to represent it as a decimal and be exact. In order to work with irrational numbers in the physical sense, the irrational numbers must be rounded and approximated.

Station 4

Students will approximate $\sqrt{99}$ in order to place it on a number line between 9 and 10. They will explain how they approximated and how they determined its placement on the number line.

Answers

1. $\sqrt{99}$

2. 9.9498743710661995473447982100121

3. 9.95

4.

5. Answers will vary, but should suggest that the irrational number needs to be rounded or truncated to one decimal place beyond the number it is being compared to, and that approximately 9.9 is much closer to 10 than to 9.

Materials List/Setup

Station 1	scientific calculator
Station 2	number cube; calculator
Station 3	calculator
Station 4	calculator

Discussion Guide

To support students in reflecting on the activities and to gather some formative information about student learning, use the following prompts to facilitate a class discussion to "debrief" the station activities.

Prompts/Questions

1. What is an irrational number?

2. Give some examples of irrational numbers.

3. How can you compare an irrational number to a rational number?

4. Where might you find irrational numbers in a real-world situation?

Think, Pair, Share

Have students jot down their own responses to questions, then discuss with a partner (who was not in their station group), and then discuss as a whole class.

Suggested Appropriate Responses

1. An irrational number is a number with a decimal that does not terminate or repeat.

2. π, $\sqrt{2}$, $\sqrt{3}$, $\sqrt{5}$, etc.

3. Round the decimal to one place value beyond the rational number you are comparing the irrational number to and determine which one is larger or smaller.

4. when building, when using the Pythagorean theorem to calculate side lengths, when calculating the volume of a cylindrical container, etc.

Possible Misunderstandings/Mistakes

- Not understanding that the irrational number π is exact when it is expressed as π and not when it is rounded to 3.14

- Incorrectly typing the square root into the calculator

- Rounding incorrectly

The Number System
Set 3: Using Rational Approximations of Irrational Numbers

Station 1

At this station you will find a calculator. Read the scenario below and answer the questions that follow.

> Alicia is babysitting for her math teacher Mrs. Ramirez's daughter. Of course, Mrs. Ramirez can't pass up the chance to assign a math problem. She asks Alicia if she would rather be paid $\$\pi$ per hour or \$3.20 per hour.

1. Use your calculator to find the number π. Write the number π with as many decimal places as you can on the line below.

   _____

2. Round your answer from problem 1 to the hundredths place. _____

3. Fill in the sentence below with "less than," "greater than," or "equal to."

   $\$\pi$ is _____ \$3.20.

4. Do you think Alicia should choose to be paid $\$\pi$ per hour or \$3.20 per hour? Why?

   _____

   _____

   _____

5. Why is π an irrational number?

   _____

   _____

6. How can you compare irrational numbers to rational numbers?

   _____

   _____

The Number System
Set 3: Using Rational Approximations of Irrational Numbers

Station 2

At this station, you will find a number cube and a calculator. Follow these steps for each problem:

- Roll the number cube. Write the result on the first line next to the problem number.

- Then, write the same number in the box under the square root symbol on the second line.

- Use your calculator to find the value of the square root of the number you rolled. Round to the nearest hundredth and write this number on the third line.

- Finally, place the original number you rolled and the square root of that number on the number line.

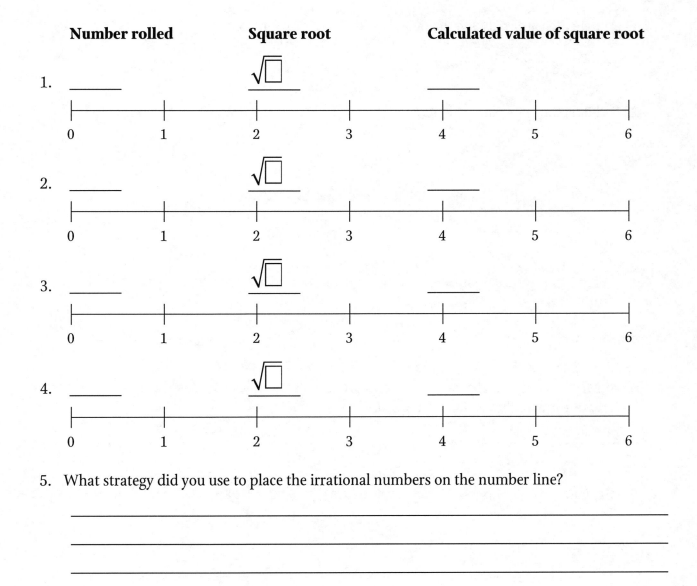

5. What strategy did you use to place the irrational numbers on the number line?

_____

_____

_____

The Number System
Set 3: Using Rational Approximations of Irrational Numbers

Station 3

Use the information below to answer the questions.

Mr. Brunelle likes to challenge his class. He tells them that they can't use any measuring tools to solve the problem that he's going to assign. He draws a square on the board and labels its side as $\sqrt{2}$ inches long. He tells the class to draw a square that is 3 times the size of this one. What will the side length of the bigger square be? Of course, the length has to be a rational number!

1. What is the approximate side length of the square, using as many decimal places as you can?

   _____

2. What is the approximate length of the side of the square rounded to the nearest tenths place?

   _____

3. What is the EXACT length of the larger square the students have to draw?

   _____

4. What is the approximate length of the square the students have to draw, rounded to the nearest tenth?

   _____

5. If Mr. Brunelle allowed you to use measuring tools, what length should you use on a ruler to create a square that is 3 times the size of the original?

   _____

6. Explain why it's impossible to draw a square with sides that are EXACTLY 3 times longer than Mr. Brunelle's square.

   _____

   _____

The Number System
Set 3: Using Rational Approximations of Irrational Numbers

Station 4

Read the scenario below and answer the questions that follow.

> Maria's teacher grades on a 10-point scale, so a 9 is an A and a 10 is an A+. Maria was amazed when she saw that her teacher had given her a $\sqrt{99}$ on her quiz on irrational numbers. Beside it was written a letter grade of A. Maria thought, "I can prove that I should get an A+!"

1. What was Maria's EXACT grade on her quiz?

   _____

2. What is an approximation of Maria's grade, using as many decimal places as you can?

   _____

3. What is Maria's grade rounded to the nearest hundredths place?

   _____

4. Plot an approximation of Maria's grade on the number line.

5. Does Maria deserve an A or an A+? Explain your reasoning.

   _____

   _____

   _____

Expressions and Equations

Set 1: Problem Solving with Exponents and Scientific Notation

Goal: To provide opportunities for students to solve problems involving exponents and scientific notation

Common Core Standards

Expressions and Equations

Work with radicals and integer exponents.

8.EE.1. Know and apply the properties of integer exponents to generate equivalent numerical expressions.

8.EE.3. Use numbers expressed in the form of a single digit times a whole-number power of 10 to estimate very large or very small quantities, and to express how many times as much one is than the other.

8.EE.4. Perform operations with numbers expressed in scientific notation, including problems where both decimal and scientific notation are used.

Student Activities Overview and Answer Key

Station 1

Students work together to solve a real-world problem involving scientific notation. Students are encouraged to brainstorm appropriate problem-solving strategies and to explain their solution process once all students in the group agree upon the solution.

Answers: Star A is 6.8×10^{13} miles from Earth.

Possible strategies: work backward; draw a diagram

Possible steps: Work backward and use division to find that Star C is 3.4×10^{17} miles from Earth, Star B is 3.4×10^{14} miles from Earth, and Star A is 6.8×10^{13} miles from Earth.

Station 2

Students work together to solve a real-world problem involving exponents. After reading the problem, students brainstorm possible problem-solving strategies. Students are encouraged to make sure everyone in the group agrees on the solution. Then students explain their solution process.

Answers: 40,960 bacteria

Possible strategies: make a table; look for a pattern

Possible steps: Make a table showing the time and the number of bacteria in the test tube. Extend the table to midnight. Alternatively, notice that the number of bacteria after n hours is $10(2)^n$ and let $n = 12$ to find the number of bacteria at midnight.

Station 3

Students work together to solve a problem involving patterns and exponents. The problem lends itself especially well to making a table and looking for a pattern. Students can also model the problem using physical objects. Students brainstorm possible strategies, solve the problem, and explain the steps of their solution method.

Answers: At Stage 10, Keisha will need 200 tiles.

Possible strategies: Make a table showing the number of the stage and the corresponding number of tiles; look for a pattern.

Possible steps: Look for patterns in the table. Extend the table to Stage 10. Alternatively, notice that at Stage n the number of tiles is $2n^2$.

Station 4

Students are given a problem about distances that are expressed in scientific notation. Students work together to brainstorm strategies they can use to solve the problem. This problem lends itself well to drawing a diagram. After solving the problem, students explain the steps of their solution.

Answers: The distance is 950 km.

Possible strategies: draw a diagram

Possible steps: Draw a diagram to show the given distances between the cities. Convert the distances from scientific notation to standard notation. The distance between Barryville and Cortez is $3200 - (150 + 2100) = 950$ km.

Materials List/Setup

Station 1	none
Station 2	none
Station 3	small square tiles or small square pieces of paper
Station 4	none

Discussion Guide

To support students in reflecting on the activities and to gather some formative information about student learning, use the following prompts to facilitate a class discussion to "debrief" the station activities.

Prompts/Questions

1. What are some different problem-solving strategies you can use to help you solve real-world problems?

2. How do you convert scientific notation to standard notation?

3. How do you divide a number in scientific notation by 1000?

4. How can you check your answer to a real-world problem?

Think, Pair, Share

Have students jot down their own responses to questions, then discuss with a partner (who was not in their station group), and then discuss as a whole class.

Suggested Appropriate Responses

1. make a table, guess and check, look for a pattern, work backward, draw a diagram, use physical objects to model the problem, etc.

2. Write the decimal part of the number's scientific-notation representation. If the exponent is positive, move the decimal point that many places right (adding zeros if needed). If the exponent is negative, move the decimal point that many places left (adding zeros if needed).

3. Since 1000 is 1×10^3, you can divide by 1000 by subtracting 3 from the exponent of 10 in the given number.

4. Reread the problem using the answer in place of the unknown quantity or quantities. Check to see if the numbers work out correctly throughout the problem.

Possible Misunderstandings/Mistakes

- Incorrectly converting scientific notation to standard notation (e.g., moving the decimal point in the wrong direction)

- Incorrectly performing arithmetic operations with numbers in scientific notation

- Confusing the use of exponents in expressions such as n^2 versus 2^n

Expressions and Equations
Set 1: Problem Solving with Exponents and Scientific Notation

Station 1

At this station, you will work with other students to solve this real-world problem.

> An astronomer is studying four stars. Star B is 5 times farther from Earth than Star A. Star C is 1000 times farther from Earth than Star B. Star D is 100 times farther from Earth than Star C. The astronomer finds that Star D is 3.4×10^{19} miles from Earth. How far is Star A from Earth?

Work with other students to discuss the problem. Brainstorm strategies you might use to solve the problem. Write the strategies below.

_____

_____

_____

Solve the problem. When everyone agrees on the answer, write it below.

_____

Explain the steps you used to solve the problem.

_____

_____

_____

_____

_____

_____

Expressions and Equations
Set 1: Problem Solving with Exponents and Scientific Notation

Station 2

At this station, you will work with other students to solve this real-world problem.

A scientist has a test tube that contains 10 bacteria at noon. The bacteria double every hour, so after one hour, the test tube contains 20 bacteria, after two hours, the test tube contains 40 bacteria, and so on. How many bacteria will be in the test tube at midnight?

Work with other students to discuss the problem. Brainstorm strategies you might use to solve the problem. Write the strategies below.

_____

_____

_____

Solve the problem. When everyone agrees on the answer, write it below.

_____

Explain the steps you used to solve the problem.

_____

_____

_____

_____

_____

_____

Expressions and Equations
Set 1: Problem Solving with Exponents and Scientific Notation

Station 3

You will find a set of tiles at this station. You may use them to help you solve this problem.

Keisha is making a pattern of tiles for a patio. The figures show the pattern at several stages. How many tiles will Keisha need to make the pattern at Stage 10?

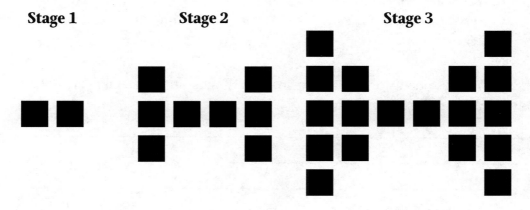

Stage 1   **Stage 2**   **Stage 3**

Work with other students to discuss the problem. Brainstorm strategies you might use to solve the problem. Write the strategies below.

_____

_____

_____

Solve the problem. When everyone agrees on the answer, write it below.

_____

What formula could you use to solve for any stage, or Stage *n*? _____

Explain the steps you used to solve the problem.

_____

_____

_____

_____

_____

_____

Expressions and Equations
Set 1: Problem Solving with Exponents and Scientific Notation

Station 4

At this station, you will work with other students to solve this real-world problem.

Four cities lie on a straight line. From west to east, the cities are Ashton, Barryville, Cortez, and Donner. The distance between Ashton and Donner is 3.2×10^3 km. The distance between Ashton and Barryville is 1.5×10^2 km, and the distance between Cortez and Donner is 2.1×10^3 km. What is the distance between Barryville and Cortez?

Work with other students to discuss the problem. Brainstorm strategies you might use to solve the problem. Write the strategies below.

_____

_____

_____

Solve the problem. When everyone agrees on the answer, write it below.

_____

Explain the steps you used to solve the problem.

_____

_____

_____

_____

_____

_____

Expressions and Equations

Set 2: Graphing Linear Equations/Solving Using Graphs

Goal: To provide opportunities for students to develop concepts and skills related to graphing a line from a table of values, *x*- and *y*-intercepts, slope-intercept form, standard form, and point-slope form. Students will also determine the slope and *x*- and *y*-intercepts given a graph or two points on the line.

Common Core Standards

Expressions and Equations

Understand the connections between proportional relationships, lines, and linear equations.

8.EE.5. Graph proportional relationships, interpreting the unit rate as the slope of the graph. Compare two different proportional relationships represented in different ways.

Student Activities Overview and Answer Key

Station 1

Students will be given dry spaghetti noodles, graph paper, and a ruler. They will construct a line using the spaghetti noodles from a table of values. They will switch the *x*- and *y*-values in the table and construct the line using spaghetti noodles to identify how this graph relates to the original graph. Then they will construct a line using spaghetti noodles given *x*- and *y*-intercepts.

Answers

1. The *x*- and *y*-values represent the coordinate pairs used to construct the graph.

2.

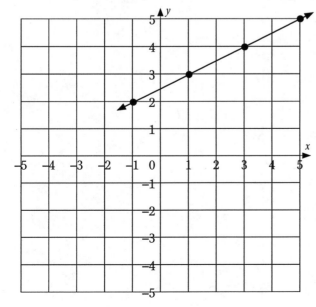

3.

x-value	*y*-value
2	−1
3	1
4	3
5	5

4.

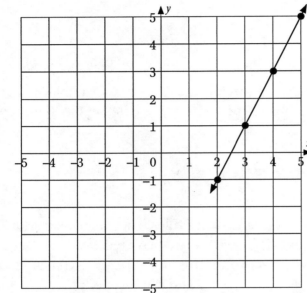

5. No, the graphs do not look the same. The coordinates are different and the slopes are ½ versus 2.

6.

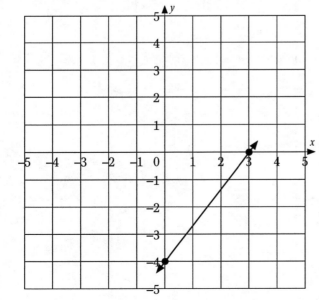

(3, 0) is the *x*-intercept.

(0, −4) is the *y*-intercept.

Station 2

Students will be given graph paper and a ruler. They complete a table of x- and y-values given equations in slope-intercept form. Then they graph these equations. They find an equation given the slope and a point on the graph. Then they graph the equation using the x- and y-intercepts.

Answers

1. Answers vary. Sample answers: (0, 3), (1, 5), (2, 7)

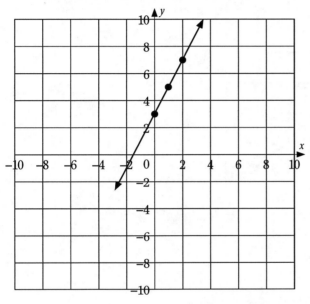

2. Answers vary. Sample answers: (–3, –4) (0, –5), (3, –6)

3.

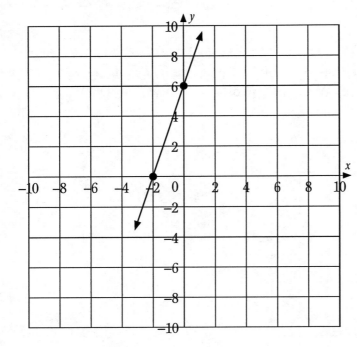

Use the *x*- and *y*-intercepts, slope, and/or point (–1, 3) to find the equation.

4. $y = 3x + 6$

5.

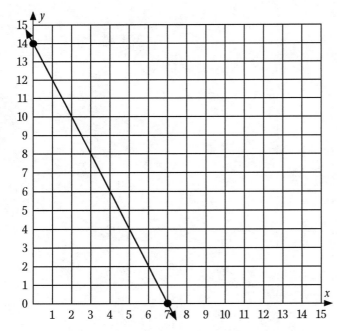

Use the *x*- and *y*-intercepts, slope, and/or point (4, 6) to find the equation.

6. $y = -2x + 14$

Station 3

Students will be given spaghetti noodles, graph paper, and a ruler. They will be given a linear equation in standard form and will rewrite it in slope-intercept form. Then they will graph the linear equation. They will be given the slope and a point on the graph and graph it using a spaghetti noodle. Then they will write the equation in point-slope form.

Answers

1. $y = -3x + 2$

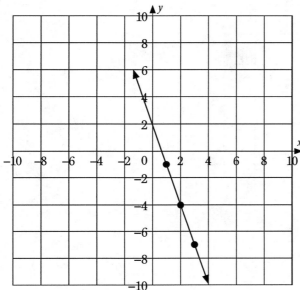

2. $y = \frac{1}{4}x - 3$

3. $y = 5x - 10$

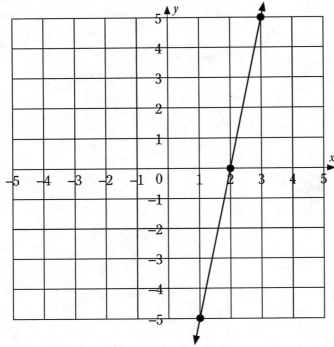

4. $y = -\frac{1}{2}x - \frac{1}{2}$

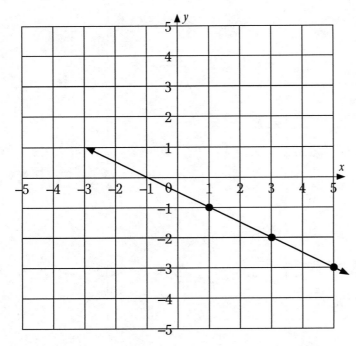

Station 4

Students will be given graph paper and a ruler. Students will determine the slope and x- and y-intercepts given a graph of a linear equation. They will construct a graph of a line given two points. Then they will find the slope and x- and y-intercepts of the line.

Answers

1. slope = 1/2; x-intercept = (2, 0); y-intercept = (0, –1)

2. slope = –1; x-intercept = (3, 0), y-intercept = (0, 3)

3. slope = 0; x-intercept = none; y-intercept = (0, 2)

4. slope = 1/2; x-intercept = (0, 0); y-intercept = (0, 0)

5. slope = –5/6; x-intercept = (8/5, 0); y-intercept = (0, 4/3)

6. slope = –4; x-intercept = (5/2, 0); y-intercept = (0, 10)

Materials List/Setup

Station 1   spaghetti noodles; graph paper; ruler

Station 2   spaghetti noodles; number cube; graph paper; ruler

Station 3   spaghetti noodles; graph paper; ruler

Station 4   graph paper; ruler

Discussion Guide

To support students in reflecting on the activities and to gather some formative information about student learning, use the following prompts to facilitate a class discussion to "debrief" the station activities.

Prompts/Questions

1. How can you find the y-value coordinate given an equation and its x-coordinate?

2. What are the definitions of the terms "x-intercept" and "y-intercept"?

3. How do you write the slope-intercept form of a linear equation?

4. How do you write the standard form of a linear equation?

5. How can you write an equation in slope-intercept form if it is given to you in standard form?

6. How can you find the equation for a line given two points on the line?

Think, Pair, Share

Have students jot down their own responses to questions, then discuss with a partner (who was not in their station group), and then discuss as a whole class.

Suggested Appropriate Responses

1. Plug the x-value into the equation and solve for the y-coordinate.

2. The x-intercept is the coordinate pair at which the graph crosses the x-axis. The y-intercept is the coordinate pair at which the graph crosses the y-axis.

3. $y = mx + b$

4. $ax + by = c$

5. Solve for y and write the equation as $y = mx + b$.

6. Find the slope of the line from the two points. Then plug in the slope and one of the points into $y - y_1 = m(x - x_1)$. Then solve for y.

Possible Misunderstandings/Mistakes

- Incorrectly plotting the coordinates in reverse order
- Not keeping track of signs when writing equations in slope-intercept and point-slope forms
- Not making sure that the y-value is 0 for the x-intercept
- Not making sure that the x-value is 0 for the y-intercept
- Incorrectly finding the slope as run/rise instead of rise/run

Expressions and Equations
Set 2: Graphing Linear Equations/Solving Using Graphs

Station 1

You will be given spaghetti noodles, graph paper, and a ruler. Use these materials and the information in the table below to answer the problems and construct the graphs.

x-value	y-value
−1	2
1	3
3	4
5	5

1. What would the x- and y-values in the table represent if you used them to graph a line?

2. Plot the table of values on your graph paper. Place the spaghetti noodles through all the points to create a line that represents the graph.

3. For each row in the table, switch the x-values with the y-values. Write the new values in the table below.

x-value	y-value

4. On the same graph, plot the table of values on your graph paper. Place the spaghetti noodles through all the points to create a line that represents the graph.

continued

Expressions and Equations
Set 2: Graphing Linear Equations/Solving Using Graphs

5. Does your graph look the same as problem 2? Why or why not?

6. A graph contains points (3, 0) and (0, –4). Use your graph paper to plot these points and construct a line through the points using the spaghetti noodles.

   These coordinates have special names.

   What is the point (3, 0) called? _____

   What is the point (0, –4) called? _____

Expressions and Equations
Set 2: Graphing Linear Equations/Solving Using Graphs

Station 2

You will be given a number cube, spaghetti noodles, graph paper, and a ruler. For problems 1 and 2, you are given an equation in slope-intercept form.

1. As a group, roll the number cube. Write the result in the first row of the *x*-value column below. Repeat this process until all the rows of the *x*-value contain a number.

   Work together to complete the table of *x*- and *y*-values based on the equation $y = 2x + 3$.

x-value	*y*-value

   As a group, graph the equation on your graph paper.

2. As a group, roll the number cube. Write the result in the first row of the *x*-values column below. Repeat this process until all the rows of the *x*-values contain a number.

   Work together to complete the table of *x*- and *y*-values based on the equation $y = -\frac{1}{3}x - 5$.

x-value	*y*-value

   As a group, graph the equation on your graph paper.

3. Use a spaghetti noodle to graph a line that has a slope of 3 and passes through the point (–1, 3). How can you use this graph to find the equation of the line?

continued

Expressions and Equations

Set 2: Graphing Linear Equations/Solving Using Graphs

4. Write the equation of this line in slope-intercept form. (*Hint*: Use $y = mx + b$.)

    _____

5. Use a spaghetti noodle to graph a line that has a slope of –2 and passes through the point (4, 6). How can you use this graph to find the equation of the line?

6. Write an equation of this line in slope-intercept form. (*Hint*: Use $y = mx + b$.)

    _____

Expressions and Equations
Set 2: Graphing Linear Equations/Solving Using Graphs

Station 3

You will be given spaghetti noodles, graph paper, and a ruler. For problems 1 and 2, you will be given an equation in standard form.

1. Work together to write the following equation in slope-intercept form: $9x + 3y = 6$

    _____

    Determine three coordinate pairs that are on the graph of $9x + 3y = 6$. Write your calculations and coordinate pairs in the space below.

    As a group, graph the equation using graph paper.

2. Work together to write the following equation in slope-intercept form: $2x - 8y = 24$

    _____

    Determine three coordinate pairs that are on the graph of $2x - 8y = 24$. Write your calculations and coordinate pairs in the space below.

    As a group, graph the equation using graph paper.

continued

Expressions and Equations
Set 2: Graphing Linear Equations/Solving Using Graphs

For problems 3 and 4, you will be given a linear equation written in point-slope form:

$$y - y_1 = m(x - x_1)$$

3. On your graph paper, use a spaghetti noodle to graph the line $y - 10 = 5(x - 4)$.

   Use the graph to find the equation of the line in slope-intercept form.

   Convert the equation from point-slope form into slope-intercept form. Show your work below.

4. On your graph paper, use a spaghetti noodle to graph the line $y + 2 = -\frac{1}{2}(x - 3)$.

   Use the graph to find the equation of the line in slope-intercept form.

   Convert the equation from point-slope form into slope-intercept form. Show your work below.

Expressions and Equations

Set 2: Graphing Linear Equations/Solving Using Graphs

Station 4

You will be given graph paper, a ruler, and graphs of linear equations. For problems 1–3, work together to determine the slope and *x*- and *y*-intercepts.

1.

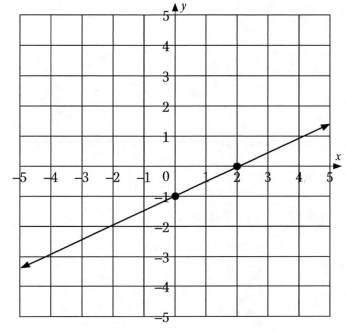

What is the slope of the graph? _____

What is the *x*-intercept? _____

What is the *y*-intercept? _____

2.

continued

Expressions and Equations
Set 2: Graphing Linear Equations/Solving Using Graphs

What is the slope of the graph? _____

What is the *x*-intercept? _____

What is the *y*-intercept? _____

3.

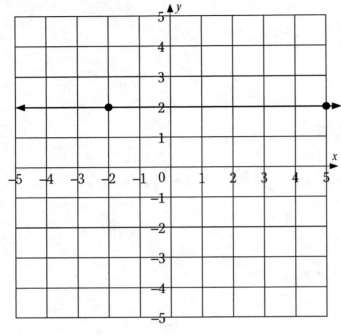

What is the slope of the graph? _____

What is the *x*-intercept? _____

What is the *y*-intercept? _____

For problems 4–6, work together to determine the slope, *x*-intercept, and *y*-intercept when given two points on the line. As a group, plot each set of two points on graph paper and construct a straight line through the points.

4. (8, 4), (12, 6)

What is the slope of the graph? _____

What is the *x*-intercept? _____

What is the *y*-intercept? _____

continued

Expressions and Equations
Set 2: Graphing Linear Equations/Solving Using Graphs

5. (–2, 3), (4, –2)

   What is the slope of the graph? _____

   What is the x-intercept? _____

   What is the y-intercept? _____

6. (1, 6), (–2, 18)

   What is the slope of the graph? _____

   What is the x-intercept? _____

   What is the y-intercept? _____

Expressions and Equations

Set 3: Writing Linear Equations

Goal: To provide opportunities for students to develop concepts and skills related to writing linear equations in slope-intercept and standard form given two points and a point and slope

Common Core Standards

Expressions and Equations

Understand the connections between proportional relationships, lines, and linear equations.

8.EE.5. Graph proportional relationships, interpreting the unit rate as the slope of the graph. Compare two different proportional relationships represented in different ways.

Student Activities Overview and Answer Key

Station 1

Students will be given spaghetti noodles, graph paper, and the general point-slope form of an equation. Students will use the spaghetti noodles to model different equations. Then they will write the slope-intercept form of an equation given the slope and y-intercept. They will also write the slope-intercept form of an equation given the y-intercept and a parallel or perpendicular equation.

Answers

1. $y = 5x + 10$
2. $y = -4x - 8$
3. $y = \dfrac{-1}{3}x + 18$
4. $y = -4x$

Station 2

Students will be given spaghetti noodles, graph paper, and the general slope-intercept and point-slope forms of a linear equation. They will determine which form of the equation to use first in order to write a linear equation when given the slope and a point on the line. They will use spaghetti noodles to model the equations. Then they will write the slope-intercept form of a line given the slope and a point on the line.

Answers

1. Use point-slope form first because you can plug in the given point for x_1 and y_1.

2. $y = 2x + 14$

3. $y = \dfrac{1}{8}x + \dfrac{95}{8}$

4. $y = -3x - 22$

5. $y = \dfrac{-2}{5}x + 14$

Station 3

Students will be given a number cube. They will use it to populate two ordered pairs. From the ordered pairs, they will find the slope and write the equation in slope-intercept form. Then they will explain how they found the slope and the equation in slope-intercept form.

Answers

1. Answers will vary.

2. Answers will vary.

3. Answers will vary.

4. Slope $= \dfrac{\text{rise}}{\text{run}} = \dfrac{y_2 - y_1}{x_2 - x_1}$

5. Find the slope from the two points. Plug one of the points and the slope into $y = mx + b$ to find b. Then write the equation in slope-intercept form.

Station 4

Students will be given 10 index cards with the following equations written on them:

$$y = 2x + 12 \qquad y = -5x - 8 \qquad y = \frac{1}{2}x + 16 \qquad y = \frac{-2}{3}x - 20 \qquad y = 10x - 24$$

$$-x + 2y = 32 \qquad 2x + 3y = -60 \qquad 4x - 2y = -24 \qquad -15x + \frac{3}{2}y = -36 \qquad \frac{-5}{2}x - \frac{1}{2}y = 4$$

They will work as a group to match the equations written in standard form with the equations written in slope-intercept form. Then they convert an equation written in standard form to slope-intercept form and vice versa.

Answers

1. $y = \dfrac{1}{2}x + 16$ and $-x + 2y = 32$

2. $y = \dfrac{-2}{3}x - 20$ and $2x + 3y = -60$

3. $y = 10x - 24$ and $-15x + \dfrac{3}{2}y = -36$

4. $4x - 2y = -24$ and $y = 2x + 12$

5. $\dfrac{-5}{2}x - \dfrac{1}{2}y = 4$ and $y = -5x - 8$

6. $y = \dfrac{1}{3}x + \dfrac{4}{3}$

7. $x - 5y = 50$

Materials List/Setup

Station 1 spaghetti noodles; graph paper

Station 2 spaghetti noodles; graph paper

Station 3 number cube

Station 4 10 index cards with the following equations written on them:

$y = 2x + 12$ $y = -5x - 8$ $y = \dfrac{1}{2}x + 16$ $y = \dfrac{-2}{3}x - 20$ $y = 10x - 24$

$-x + 2y = 32$ $2x + 3y = -60$ $4x - 2y = -24$ $-15x + \dfrac{3}{2}y = -36$ $\dfrac{-5}{2}x - \dfrac{1}{2}y = 4$

Discussion Guide

To support students in reflecting on the activities and to gather some formative information about student learning, use the following prompts to facilitate a class discussion to "debrief" the station activities.

Prompts/Questions

1. How do you write the standard form of a linear equation?
2. How do you write the slope-intercept form of a linear equation?
3. How do you write the slope-intercept form of a linear equation given a point and the slope?
4. How do you write the slope-intercept form of a linear equation given two points on the line?
5. How do you convert the standard form of a linear equation into slope-intercept form?
6. How do you convert the slope-intercept form of a linear equation into standard form?

Think, Pair, Share

Have students jot down their own responses to questions, then discuss with a partner (who was not in their station group), and then discuss as a whole class.

Suggested Appropriate Responses

1. $ax + by = c$
2. $y = mx + b$
3. Use the point-slope form of the equation to plug in the given point and slope. Then write the equation in slope-intercept form.
4. Find the slope from the two points. Plug one of the points and the slope into $y = mx + b$ to find b. Then write the equation in slope-intercept form.
5. Solve for y.
6. Move the x-value to the left-hand side of the equation by using either the addition or subtraction property of equality and make sure that the coefficients are whole numbers with the coefficient of x being positive.

Possible Misunderstandings/Mistakes

- Mixing up the x- and y-values when plugging them into the point-slope or slope-intercept forms
- Not keeping track of positive and negative signs when converting from standard form to slope-intercept form and vice versa
- Incorrectly finding the slope as $\frac{run}{rise}$ instead of $\frac{rise}{run}$

Expressions and Equations
Set 3: Writing Linear Equations

Station 1

You will find spaghetti noodles and graph paper at this station. Draw a coordinate plane on your graph paper by creating and labeling the x-axis and the y-axis. For each problem, use the given information and the spaghetti to find the slope-intercept form of the equation.

- Slope-intercept form is written as $y = mx + b$.

1. The equation has a y-intercept of $(0, 10)$ and a slope of 5.

   Model this equation using the spaghetti. Then write the equation in slope-intercept form.

2. The equation has a y-intercept of $(0, -8)$ and is parallel to the line $y = -4x - 16$.

   Model this equation using the spaghetti. Then write the equation in slope-intercept form.

3. The equation has a y-intercept of 18 and is perpendicular to the line $y = 3x + 9$.

   Model this equation using the spaghetti. Then write the equation in slope-intercept form.

4. The graph of the equation passes through the origin and is perpendicular to $y = \dfrac{1}{4}x$.

   Model this equation using the spaghetti. Then write the equation in slope-intercept form.

Expressions and Equations
Set 3: Writing Linear Equations

Station 2

You will find spaghetti noodles and graph paper at this station. Draw a coordinate plane on your graph paper by creating and labeling the *x*-axis and the *y*-axis. Use the spaghetti and what you know about the slope-intercept and point-slope forms of a linear equation to answer the questions.

- Slope-intercept form is written as $y = mx + b$.
- Point-slope form is written as $y - y_1 = m(x - x_1)$.

1. You want to find a linear equation. Which form should you use first if you are given the slope and a point on the line?

2. Use spaghetti to model a line that has a slope of 2 and passes through (–3, 8). Then write the equation for this line in slope-intercept form.

3. Use spaghetti to model a line that has a slope of $\frac{1}{8}$ and passes through (1, 12). Then write the equation for this line in slope-intercept form.

4. Use spaghetti to model a line that has a slope of –3 and passes through (–4, –10). Then write the equation for this line in slope-intercept form.

5. Use spaghetti to model a line that has a slope of $-\frac{2}{5}$ and passes through (–15, 20). Then write the equation for this line in slope-intercept form.

Expressions and Equations
Set 3: Writing Linear Equations

Station 3

You will be given a number cube. For each problem, roll the number cube four times to create two ordered pairs. Then use these ordered pairs to find the slope and write the equation in slope-intercept form.

- Slope-intercept form is written as $y = mx + b$.

1. First ordered pair: (,   )

    Second ordered pair: (,   )

    Slope = _____

    Equation written in slope-intercept form: _____

2. First ordered pair: (,   )

    Second ordered pair: (,   )

    Slope = _____

    Equation written in slope-intercept form: _____

3. First ordered pair: (,   )

    Second ordered pair: (,   )

    Slope = _____

    Equation written in slope-intercept form: _____

4. How did you find the slope from the two ordered pairs?

5. How did you find b in the slope-intercept form of the equation?

Expressions and Equations
Set 3: Writing Linear Equations

Station 4

At this station, you will find 10 index cards with the following equations written on them:

$$y = 2x + 12 \qquad y = -5x - 8 \qquad y = \frac{1}{2}x + 16 \qquad y = \frac{-2}{3}x - 20 \qquad y = 10x - 24$$

$$-x + 2y = 32 \qquad 2x + 3y = -60 \qquad 4x - 2y = -24 \qquad -15x + \frac{3}{2}y = -36 \qquad \frac{-5}{2}x - \frac{1}{2}y = 4$$

As a group, shuffle the cards. Work as a group to match the linear equation written in standard form with the same equation written in slope-intercept form. Write your matches on the lines below.

1. _____

2. _____

3. _____

4. _____

5. _____

6. Rewrite the equation $-3x + 9y = 12$ so that it's in slope-intercept form. Show your work.

7. Rewrite the equation $y = \frac{1}{5}x - 10$ so that it's in standard form. Show your work.

Expressions and Equations

Set 4: Solving 2-by-2 Systems by Graphing

Goal: To provide opportunities for students to develop concepts and skills related to solving linear systems of equations by graphing

Common Core Standards

Expressions and Equations

8.EE.8.   Analyze and solve pairs of simultaneous linear equations.

   a.   Understand that solutions to a system of two linear equations in two variables correspond to points of intersection of their graphs, because points of intersection satisfy both equations simultaneously.

   b.   Solve systems of two linear equations in two variables algebraically, and estimate solutions by graphing the equations. Solve simple cases by inspection.

   c.   Solve real-world and mathematical problems leading to two linear equations in two variables.

Student Activities Overview and Answer Key

Station 1

Students will be given graph paper and a ruler. Students will graph a system of linear equations. They will find the point of intersection of the lines and realize that this is the solution to the linear system. They will double-check the point of intersection by substituting it into the original equations.

Answers

1.

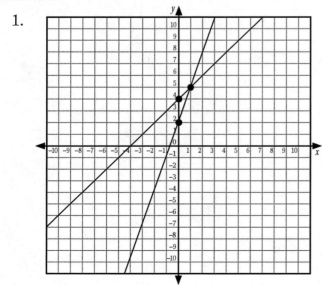

2. Yes, (1, 5)

3. The point of intersection is the solution of the system of linear equations.

4. Substitute (1, 5) into both equations to verify that it satisfies both equations.

5.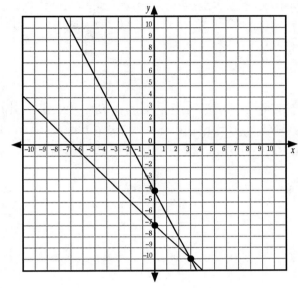

6. (3, −10)

Station 2

Students will be given four index cards with the following systems of linear equations written on them:

$$\begin{cases} 10x - 2y = 10 \\ 5x - y = 5 \end{cases} ; \begin{cases} x - y = 3 \\ 2x - y = 5 \end{cases} ; \begin{cases} y = 4 \\ -x + y = 10 \end{cases} ; \begin{cases} y = 2x + 5 \\ -2x + y = 8 \end{cases}$$

Students will work together to match each system of linear equations with the appropriate graph. They will explain the strategy they used to match the graphs.

Answers

1. $\begin{cases} 5x + y = -3 \\ 7x + y = -5 \end{cases}$

2. $\begin{cases} y = 4 \\ -x + y = 10 \end{cases}$

3. $\begin{cases} 10x - 2y = 10 \\ 5x - y = 5 \end{cases}$

4. $\begin{cases} y = 2x + 5 \\ -2x + y = 8 \end{cases}$

5. Answers will vary. Possible answer: Finding the point of intersection of the lines. This is the solution to the linear system. Substitute this point into the equations to see which systems of linear equations have this solution.

Station 3

Students will be given linear equations and will find points that satisfy the equations. Then they will look at the equations as a linear system. They will find the solution, or no solution, of the linear system. They will describe the strategy they used to determine the solution of the linear system.

Answers

1.

x	y
–5	–14
0	–4
5	6
10	16
15	26

2.

x	y
–4	37
0	31
8	19
10	16
12	13

3. Yes, (10, 16)

4. They had the same ordered pair of (10, 16), which means the lines intersect at that point.

5.

x	y
–2	6
0	10
2	14
4	18

Expressions and Equations
Set 4: Solving 2-by-2 Systems by Graphing

Instruction

6.

x	y
−2	−14
0	−10
2	−6
4	−2

7. The table of values may or may not contain the solution.

8. You can use the slope of each line and *y*-intercepts, or you can graph the equations and see if they intersect.

9. There is no solution. Each equation has the same slope, but different *y*-intercepts.

Station 4

Students will be given a graphing calculator. Students will be shown how to find the solution of a system of linear equations using the graphing calculator. Then they will use the graphing calculator to find the solutions of given systems of linear equations.

Answers

1. (−1.67, −9.67)

2. (−8, −12)

3. (1.29, 3.86)

4. (0.73, 3.27)

Materials List/Setup

Station 1   graph paper; ruler

Station 2   four index cards with the following systems of linear equations written on them:

$$\begin{cases} 10x - 2y = 10 \\ 5x - y = 5 \end{cases} ; \begin{cases} 5x + y = -3 \\ 7x + y = -5 \end{cases} ; \begin{cases} y = 4 \\ -x + y = 10 \end{cases} ; \begin{cases} y = 2x + 5 \\ -2x + y = 8 \end{cases}$$

Station 3   none

Station 4   graphing calculator

Discussion Guide

To support students in reflecting on the activities and to gather some formative information about student learning, use the following prompts to facilitate a class discussion to "debrief" the station activities.

Prompts/Questions

1. How do you solve systems of linear equations by graphing?

2. How do you know if a system of linear equations has infinite solutions?

3. How do you know if a system of linear equations has no solutions?

4. How can you use a graphing calculator to graph and solve systems of linear equations?

5. Give an example of a graph of a linear system that is used in the real world.

Think, Pair, Share

Have students jot down their own responses to questions, then discuss with a partner (who was not in their station group), and then discuss as a whole class.

Suggested Appropriate Responses

1. Graph each line. Their point of intersection is the solution to the linear system.

2. Graph each line. If the lines are the same line then they have infinite solutions. Or, if the lines have the same slope and y-intercept, then there are infinite solutions.

3. Graph each line. If the lines are parallel or have no point of intersection, the system has no solutions.

4. Type the equations into Y1 and Y2. Hit "GRAPH", "2nd", "Trace", and select "5: Intersect". Then hit the "ENTER" key three times to find the point of intersection. The point of intersection is the solution to the linear system.

5. Answers will vary. Possible answer: comparing service plans from two different cell phone companies

Possible Misunderstandings/Mistakes

- Incorrectly graphing the equations by not finding the correct slope and intercepts

- Not realizing that equations with the same slope and y-intercept are the same line. If they are a system of linear equations then the system has infinite solutions.

- Not realizing that parallel lines have no solutions

- Not realizing the point of intersection of the two lines is the solution to the system of linear equations

Expressions and Equations
Set 4: Solving 2-by-2 Systems by Graphing

Station 1

At this station, you will find graph paper and a ruler. You can find the solution to a system of linear equations by graphing each equation in the same coordinate plane.

1. As a group, graph each of the following linear equations on the same graph.

   $y = 3x + 2$

   $y = x + 4$

2. Do the lines intersect? If so, find the point at which the two lines intersect.

3. What does this point of intersection tell you about the two equations?

4. How can you double-check your answer to problem 3?

5. As a group, graph the system of linear equations on a new graph.

   $\begin{cases} y = -2x - 4 \\ y = -x - 7 \end{cases}$

6. Using this graph, what is the solution to the linear system?

Expressions and Equations

Set 4: Solving 2-by-2 Systems by Graphing

Station 2

At this station, you will find four index cards with the following linear systems of equations written on them:

$$\begin{cases} 10x - 2y = 10 \\ 5x - y = 5 \end{cases} ; \begin{cases} 5x + y = -3 \\ 7x + y = -5 \end{cases} ; \begin{cases} y = 4 \\ -x + y = 10 \end{cases} ; \begin{cases} y = 2x + 5 \\ -2x + y = 8 \end{cases}$$

Work together to match each system of linear equations with the appropriate graph below. Write the appropriate system of linear equations under each graph.

1.

Answer: _____

2.

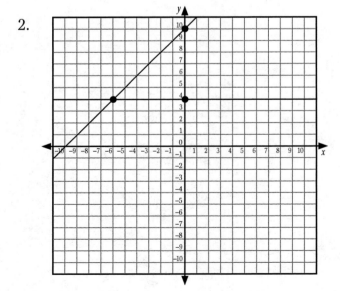

Answer: _____

continued

Expressions and Equations
Set 4: Solving 2-by-2 Systems by Graphing

3.

Answer: _____

4.

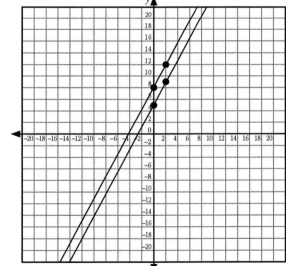

Answer: _____

5. What strategy did you use to match the systems of linear equations with the appropriate graph?

Station Activities for Common Core Mathematics, Grade 8

Expressions and Equations
Set 4: Solving 2-by-2 Systems by Graphing

Station 3

Use what you know about linear equations to answer the questions.

1. Complete the table below for the linear equation $2x - y = 4$.

x	y
−5	
0	
5	
10	
15	

2. Complete the table below for the linear equation $3x + 2y = 62$.

x	y
−4	
0	
8	
10	
12	

3. If $\begin{cases} 2x - y = 4 \\ 3x + 2y = 62 \end{cases}$ were a set of linear equations, would the set have a solution?

   If so, what is the solution?

4. What strategy did you use in problem 3 to find your answer?

5. Complete the table below for the linear equation $2x = y - 10$.

x	y
−2	
0	
2	
4	

continued

Expressions and Equations
Set 4: Solving 2-by-2 Systems by Graphing

6. Complete the table below for the linear equation $2x = y + 10$.

x	y
–2	
0	
2	
4	

7. If $\begin{cases} 2x = y - 10 \\ 2x = y + 10 \end{cases}$ were a set of linear equations, why would you need more information than just the values in the tables you found for problems 5 and 6 to determine any solutions?

8. What information would you need to determine whether or not a system of linear equations has a solution, infinite solutions, or no solutions?

9. Does $\begin{cases} 2x = y - 10 \\ 2x = y + 10 \end{cases}$ have a solution? Why or why not?

Expressions and Equations
Set 4: Solving 2-by-2 Systems by Graphing

Station 4

At this station, you will find a graphing calculator. You can graph systems of linear equations on your calculator to find their point of intersection. Work together to graph systems of linear equations on your calculator.

Given: $\begin{cases} y = 4x - 3 \\ y = x - 8 \end{cases}$

> Follow these steps on your graphing calculator to find the point of intersection for this system of equations:
>
> 1. Hit the "Y =" key. Type Y1 = $4x - 3$.
>
> 2. Type Y2 = $x - 8$.
>
> 3. Hit the "GRAPH" key.
>
> 4. Hit "2nd" and then "TRACE". Select "5: Intersect".
>
> 5. Hit "ENTER" three times. You will be given the x- and y-values of the intersection.

1. What is the intersection/solution of $\begin{cases} y = 4x - 3 \\ y = x - 8 \end{cases}$? _____

Using the same steps, find the solution to each system of linear equations below on your graphing calculator.

2. $\begin{cases} y = 3x + 12 \\ y = x - 4 \end{cases}$

   Solution = _____

3. $\begin{cases} y = -4x + 9 \\ y = 3x \end{cases}$

   Solution = _____

4. $\begin{cases} 2x + 2y = 8 \\ y = 10x - 4 \end{cases}$

   Solution = _____

Expressions and Equations

Set 5: Solving 2-by-2 Systems by Substitution

Instruction

Goal: To provide opportunities for students to develop concepts and skills related to solving systems of linear equations using substitution

Common Core Standards

Expressions and Equations

8.EE.8. Analyze and solve pairs of simultaneous linear equations.

   a. Understand that solutions to a system of two linear equations in two variables correspond to points of intersection of their graphs, because points of intersection satisfy both equations simultaneously.

   b. Solve systems of two linear equations in two variables algebraically, and estimate solutions by graphing the equations. Solve simple cases by inspection.

   c. Solve real-world and mathematical problems leading to two linear equations in two variables.

Student Activities Overview and Answer Key

Station 1

Students will be given 10 blue algebra tiles to represent the coefficient of x, 10 yellow algebra tiles to represent the coefficient of y, and 40 red algebra tiles to represent the constant. They will also be given index cards with x, y, $+$, $-$, and $=$ written on them.

    Students use the algebra tiles and index cards to model a system of linear equations. They rearrange the tiles and index cards to solve for x. Then they solve for y to find the solution to the system of linear equations.

Answers

1. x and y

2. $x = -y + 10$

3. $2(-y + 10) + y = 15; y = 5$

4. Substitute y into the first equation to find $x = 5$.

5. $x + y = 10$ and $5 + 5 = 10$; $2x + y = 15$ and $2(5) + 5 = 15$

Station 2

Students will be given systems of linear equations. They will work together to solve each system of linear equations using the substitution method. They will show their work and explain how to double-check their answers.

Answers

1. $x = y + 3$

    $5(y + 3) - y = -5$

    $5y + 15 - y = -5$

    $y = -5$

    and

    $5x - (-5) = -5$

    $x = -2$

2. For $5x = 4y + 1$, $x = \dfrac{4}{5}y + \dfrac{1}{5}$, so $7\left(\dfrac{4}{5}y + \dfrac{1}{5}\right) + 4y = 11$, $y = 1$ and for

    $5x - 4(1) = 1$, $x = 1$.

3. Solve for one variable in the first equation. Substitute this quantity in for that variable in the second equation. Solve for the variable still in the equation. Then substitute your answer for that variable into the original equation to find the value of the other variable.

4. Substitute x and y into both equations to make sure they satisfy both equations.

5. You substitute one variable in terms of the other variable to find x or y.

Station 3

Students will be given a system of linear equations and nine index cards with the following equations written on them:

$10x = 30$	$y = 1$	$2x - 12x + 30 = 0$	$y = 2x - 5$	$-10x + 30 = 0$
$6 - y = 5$	$x = 3$	$2x - 6(2x - 5) = 0$	$2(3) - y = 5$	

Each index card represents a step in solving a system of linear equations by substitution. Students work together to arrange the steps in the correct order. They give the strategy they used to arrange the index cards.

Answers

1. $y = 2x - 5$

2. $2x - 6(2x - 5) = 0$

3. $2x - 12x + 30 = 0$

4. $-10x + 30 = 0$

5. $10x = 30$

6. $x = 3$

7. $2(3) - y = 5$

8. $6 - y = 5$

9. $y = 1$

10. Answers will vary. Possible answer: I looked for one variable written in terms of the other variable. Then I solved by substitution in a step-by-step manner.

Station 4

Students will be given systems of linear equations that have either infinite solutions or no solutions. They will try to find the solution of the system. Then they will realize that lines with the same slope and y-intercept have infinite solutions. They will also find that lines that have the same slope but different y-intercepts have no solutions.

Answers

1. $y = 4 - x$
   $2x + 2(4 - x) = 8$
   $8 = 8$

2. Answers will vary.

3. -1

4. -1

5. yes; yes

6. When lines are parallel and have the same y-intercept, they are the same line. This means the system of linear equations has an infinite number of solutions.

7. $4 \neq 10$

8. no solutions

9. 2

10. 2

11. yes

12. no

13. The lines have the same slope, but different y-intercepts. There are no solutions to the system of linear equations.

Materials List/Setup

Station 1 10 blue algebra tiles to represent the coefficient of x, 10 yellow algebra tiles to represent the coefficient of y, and 40 red algebra tiles to represent the constant; index cards with x, y, $+$, $-$, and $=$ written on them

Station 2 none

Station 3 nine index cards with the following written on them:

$10x = 30$	$y = 1$	$2x - 12x + 30 = 0$	$y = 2x - 5$	$-10x + 30 = 0$
$6 - y = 5$	$x = 3$	$2x - 6(2x - 5) = 0$	$2(3) - y = 5$	

Station 4 none

Discussion Guide

To support students in reflecting on the activities and to gather some formative information about student learning, use the following prompts to facilitate a class discussion to "debrief" the station activities.

Prompts/Questions

1. How do you solve systems of linear equations using substitution?

2. How many solutions does a system of linear equations have if the equations have the same slope and y-intercept?

3. How many solutions does a system of linear equations have if the equations have the same slope, but different y-intercepts?

4. Why does the "substitution method" have this name?

Think, Pair, Share

Have students jot down their own responses to questions, then discuss with a partner (who was not in their station group), and then discuss as a whole class.

Suggested Appropriate Responses

1. Solve for one variable in the first equation. Substitute this quantity in for that variable in the second equation. Solve for the variable still in the equation. Then substitute your answer for that variable into the original equation to find the value of the other variable.

2. infinite number of solutions

3. no solutions

4. You substitute one variable in terms of the other variable to find x or y.

Possible Misunderstandings/Mistakes

- Incorrectly solving for one variable when rewriting an equation in step 1 of the process

- Incorrectly substituting x in the first equation for y in the second equation

- Not double checking that the values of x and y satisfy both equations

- Not realizing that lines that have the same slope and y-intercept are actually the same line. These have an infinite number of solutions to the system of linear equations.

- Not realizing that parallel lines that have different y-intercepts will have no solutions for the system of linear equations

Expressions and Equations
Set 5: Solving 2-by-2 Systems by Substitution

Station 1

At this station, you will find 10 blue algebra tiles to represent the coefficient of x, 10 yellow algebra tiles to represent the coefficient of y, and 40 red algebra tiles to represent the constant. You will also be given index cards with x, y, +, −, and = written on them.

As a group, arrange the algebra tiles and index cards to model the system of linear equations below:

$$\begin{cases} x + y = 10 \\ 2x + y = 15 \end{cases}$$

1. What values do you need to find in order to solve this system of linear equations?

2. Rearrange $x + y = 10$ to solve for x. Write your answer on the line below.

   _____

3. Substitute what you found in problem 2 into the equation $2x + y = 15$. Show your work in the space below.

   Now solve for y. What is the value of y?

   _____

4. How can you use this value of y to find x?

   What is the value of x?

   _____

5. Verify that x and y satisfy both equations. Show your work in the space below.

Expressions and Equations
Set 5: Solving 2-by-2 Systems by Substitution

Station 2

Use substitution to find the solutions for each system of linear equations. Show your work.

1. $\begin{cases} 5x - y = -5 \\ x - y = 3 \end{cases}$

2. $\begin{cases} 5x - 4y = 1 \\ 7x + 4y = 11 \end{cases}$

3. What strategies did you use to find x and y?

4. How can you double-check your solutions for x and y?

5. Why is this method called the "substitution" method?

Expressions and Equations
Set 5: Solving 2-by-2 Systems by Substitution

Station 3

At this station, you will find nine index cards with the following written on them:

$10x = 30$ $y = 1$ $2x - 12x + 30 = 0$ $y = 2x - 5$ $-10x + 30 = 0$

$6 - y = 5$ $x = 3$ $2x - 6(2x - 5) = 0$ $2(3) - y = 5$

Given: $\begin{cases} 2x - y = 5 \\ 2x - 6y = 0 \end{cases}$

    Each index card represents one step in solving the linear system of equations by substitution. Shuffle the index cards. Work together to arrange the index cards in the correct order of solving the system of linear equations by substitution.

List the steps below.

1. _____

2. _____

3. _____

4. _____

5. _____

6. _____

7. _____

8. _____

9. _____

10. What strategy did you use to find the order of the steps?

Expressions and Equations

Set 5: Solving 2-by-2 Systems by Substitution

Station 4

Work as a group to solve this system of linear equations by substitution.

$$\begin{cases} x + y = 4 \\ 2x + 2y = 8 \end{cases}$$

1. What happens when you solve this equation by substitution?

2. Based on problem 1, how many solutions do you think this system of linear equations has?
   _____

3. What is the slope of $x + y = 4$? _____

4. What is the slope of $2x + 2y = 8$? _____

5. Are these two lines parallel? _____

   Do these lines have the same y-intercept? _____

6. How can you relate the slopes and y-intercepts of each equation to the number of solutions for the linear system of equations?

continued

Expressions and Equations
Set 5: Solving 2-by-2 Systems by Substitution

Work as a group to solve this system of linear equations by substitution.

$$\begin{cases} y = 2x + 4 \\ y = 2x + 10 \end{cases}$$

7. What happens when you solve this equation by substitution?

8. Based on problem 7, how many solutions do you think this system of linear equations has?

    _____

9. What is the slope of $y = 2x + 4$? _____

10. What is the slope of $y = 2x + 10$? _____

11. Are these two lines parallel? _____

12. Do these lines have the same y-intercept? _____

13. How can you relate the slopes and y-intercepts of each equation to the number of solutions for the linear system of equations?

Expressions and Equations

Set 6: Solving 2-by-2 Systems by Elimination

Goal: To provide opportunities for students to develop concepts and skills related to solving systems of linear equations using multiplication and addition

Common Core Standards

Expressions and Equations

Analyze and solve linear equations and pairs of simultaneous linear equations.

8.EE.8. Analyze and solve pairs of simultaneous linear equations.

    a. Understand that solutions to a system of two linear equations in two variables correspond to points of intersection of their graphs, because points of intersection satisfy both equations simultaneously.

    b. Solve systems of two linear equations in two variables algebraically, and estimate solutions by graphing the equations. Solve simple cases by inspection.

    c. Solve real-world and mathematical problems leading to two linear equations in two variables.

Student Activities Overview and Answer Key

Station 1

Students will be given an equation. Students will use the addition property to solve the equation. Then they will apply the addition property to a system of linear equations.

Answers

1. Combine like terms $(x + x)$. Subtract 6 from both sides or add −6 to both sides of the equation using the addition property.

2. $x = 4$

3. y because you have $-1y + 1y = 0y$

4. $2x = 16$, so $x = 8$

5. $y = 3$

6. $(8, 3)$

7. $3y = 24$, so $y = 8$; $x = 1$; $(1, 8)$

8. $-2y = 18$, so $y = -9$; $x = -1$; $(-1, -9)$

Station 2

Students will be given 10 yellow, 10 red, and 20 green algebra tiles. Students are also given index cards with the symbols x, y, $-$, $+$, and $=$ written on them. They will use the algebra tiles and index cards to model and solve systems of linear equations by using the addition/elimination method.

Answers

1. yellow algebra tiles

2. red algebra tiles

3. Student drawings should show 7 yellow tiles $(7x) = 14$ green tiles.

4. $x = 2$

5. Substitute x into the first equation to solve for y.

6. $(2, 1)$

7. $(2, 16)$

Station 3

Students will be given a system of linear equations. They solve the system using multiplication and addition on the x variable in the elimination method. Then they solve the same systems using multiplication and addition on the y variable in the elimination method.

Answers

1. No, because the same variable must have opposite coefficients in the two equations.

2. -2

3. $4x + 10y = 42$

   $-4x - 2y = -10$

   $8y = 32$

   $y = 4$

4. $4x + 10(4) = 42$

   $x = \frac{1}{2}$; solution is $(\frac{1}{2}, 4)$

5. $4x + 10y = 42$

   $-20x - 10y = -50$

   $x = \frac{1}{2}$, so $y = 4$; solution is $(\frac{1}{2}, 4)$

Station 4

Students will be given eight index cards with the following written on them:

$$5x = 0 \qquad (0, 4) \qquad x = 0 \qquad -11y = -44 \qquad 5x + 2(4) = 8 \qquad y = 4$$

$$\begin{cases} 10x + 4y = 16 \\ -10x - 15y = -60 \end{cases} \qquad \begin{cases} 2(5x + 2y) = 2(8) \\ -5(2x + 3y) = -5(12) \end{cases}$$

Students work together to arrange the index cards to reflect how to find the solution of the system of linear equations. Then they explain the strategy they used to find this order.

Answers

1. $\begin{cases} 2(5x + 2y) = 2(8) \\ -5(2x + 3y) = -5(12) \end{cases}$

2. $\begin{cases} 10x + 4y = 16 \\ -10x - 15y = -60 \end{cases}$

3. $-11y = -44$

4. $y = 4$

5. $5x + 2(4) = 8$

6. $5x = 0$

7. $x = 0$

8. $(0, 4)$

9. Answers will vary. Possible answers: We figured out which variable was going to be multiplied and added to cancel it out. Then we figured out the rest of the steps from this information.

Materials List/Setup

Station 1 none

Station 2 10 yellow, 10 red, and 20 green algebra tiles; index cards with the symbols x, y, $-$, $+$, and $=$ written on them

Station 3 none

Station 4 eight index cards with the following written on them:

$$5x = 0 \qquad (0, 4) \qquad x = 0 \qquad -11y = -44 \qquad 5x + 2(4) = 8 \qquad y = 4$$

$$\begin{cases} 10x + 4y = 16 \\ -10x - 15y = -60 \end{cases} \qquad \begin{cases} 2(5x + 2y) = 2(8) \\ -5(2x + 3y) = -5(12) \end{cases}$$

Expressions and Equations
Set 6: Solving 2-by-2 Systems by Elimination

Discussion Guide

To support students in reflecting on the activities and to gather some formative information about student learning, use the following prompts to facilitate a class discussion to "debrief" the station activities.

Prompts/Questions

1. How do you solve a system of linear equations by addition?

2. What is an example of a system of linear equations that you can solve by addition?

3. How do you solve a system of linear equations by multiplication and addition?

4. What is an example of a system of linear equations that you can solve by multiplication and addition?

5. Does it matter which variable you cancel out through multiplication and/or addition? Why or why not?

6. What type of relationship must the same variable in each equation have before you can cancel that variable?

Think, Pair, Share

Have students jot down their own responses to questions, then discuss with a partner (who was not in their station group), and then discuss as a whole class.

Suggested Appropriate Responses

1. Add the same variable in both equations to cancel it out. Solve for the other variable. Then solve for the original variable.

2. Answers will vary. Possible answer: $\begin{cases} x + 2y = 4 \\ x - 2y = 10 \end{cases}$

3. Multiply the same variable in each equation so they have coefficients of opposite values. Then use addition to cancel out that variable. Solve for the other variable. Then solve for the original variable.

4. Answers will vary. Possible answer: $\begin{cases} -2x + y = 2 \\ x + 2y = 10 \end{cases}$

5. No, it doesn't matter. You will arrive at the same answer.

6. The same variable must have opposite coefficients in the two equations.

Possible Misunderstandings/Mistakes

- Not making sure that the same variable has opposite coefficients in both equations before canceling it out

- When using multiplication, forgetting to apply it to all terms in the equation

- Selecting the wrong multipliers to multiply by each equation in order to cancel out a variable

- Trying to solve the system without canceling out a variable through the elimination method

Expressions and Equations
Set 6: Solving 2-by-2 Systems by Elimination

Station 1

Use what you know about systems of linear equations to answer the questions.

1. How do you solve the equation $x + x + 6 = 14$?

2. What is the solution to this equation? _____

You can apply this same technique when solving systems of linear equations.

Given: $\begin{cases} x + y = 11 \\ x - y = 5 \end{cases}$

You can add these equations together by adding like terms.

3. Which variable would cancel out? Explain your answer.

4. In the space below, rewrite the variable and constant that is left after adding the two equations together. Then solve for that variable.

    _____

5. What is the value of the other variable?

    _____

6. What is the solution to $\begin{cases} x + y = 11 \\ x - y = 5 \end{cases}$?

    _____

continued

Expressions and Equations

Set 6: Solving 2-by-2 Systems by Elimination

As a group, solve the following systems of linear equations using this addition method. Show your work.

7. $\begin{cases} 2x + y = 10 \\ -2x + 2y = 14 \end{cases}$

8. $\begin{cases} -x - y = 10 \\ x - y = 8 \end{cases}$

Expressions and Equations
Set 6: Solving 2-by-2 Systems by Elimination

Station 2

At this station, you will find 10 yellow, 10 red, and 20 green algebra tiles. You will also be given index cards with the symbols x, y, $-$, $+$, and $=$ written on them.

Use the yellow algebra tiles to represent the coefficient of x. Use the red algebra tiles to represent the coefficient of y. Use the green algebra tiles to represent the constant.

As a group, arrange the algebra tiles and the x, y, $-$, $+$, and $=$ index cards to model the following system of linear equations:

$$\begin{cases} 3x + 2y = 8 \\ 4x - 2y = 6 \end{cases}$$

To solve this system of linear equations you add the two equations.

1. Which algebra tiles will be added together?

   _____

2. Which algebra tiles will cancel each other out?

   _____

3. Arrange the algebra tiles to model the new equation you found. Draw a picture of this equation in the space below.

4. Move the algebra tiles around to solve for the remaining variable. What is this variable and its solution?

   _____

continued

Expressions and Equations

Set 6: Solving 2-by-2 Systems by Elimination

5. How can you find the value of the other variable?

6. What is the solution to this system of linear equations?

   _____

7. Use your algebra tiles to model and solve the following system of linear equations. Write your answer in the space below.

$$\begin{cases} -3x + y = 10 \\ 3x + y = 22 \end{cases}$$

Expressions and Equations
Set 6: Solving 2-by-2 Systems by Elimination

Station 3

Using the elimination method to solve a system of equations means that you eliminate one variable so you can solve for the other variable. Use this information to answer the questions about the following system of equations:

$$\begin{cases} 4x + 10y = 42 \\ 2x + y = 5 \end{cases}$$

1. Can you eliminate a variable from the system of equations above given the form it is written in? Why or why not?

2. What number can you multiply x by in the second equation in order to cancel out the x variable?

   _____

3. Cancel out the x variable and solve for y. Show your work. Remember to keep both sides of the equation balanced.

4. Solve for x. What is the solution to this system of equations? _____

5. Find the solution for the same system $\begin{cases} 4x + 10y = 42 \\ 2x + y = 5 \end{cases}$, but this time eliminate the y variable first. Show your work.

Station Activities for Common Core Mathematics, Grade 8

Expressions and Equations
Set 6: Solving 2-by-2 Systems by Elimination

Station 4

At this station, you will find eight index cards with the following written on them:

$$5x = 0 \qquad (0, 4) \qquad x = 0 \qquad -11y = -44 \qquad 5x + 2(4) = 8 \qquad y = 4$$

$$\begin{cases} 10x + 4y = 16 \\ -10x - 15y = -60 \end{cases} \qquad \begin{cases} 2(5x + 2y) = 2(8) \\ -5(2x + 3y) = -5(12) \end{cases}$$

Each index card represents a step in solving a system of linear equations. Shuffle the index cards. Work as a group to arrange the index cards in the correct order to solve the following system of linear equations:

$$\begin{cases} 5x + 2y = 8 \\ 2x + 3y = 12 \end{cases}$$

Write the steps on the lines below.

1. _____

2. _____

3. _____

4. _____

5. _____

6. _____

7. _____

8. _____

9. What strategy did you use to arrange the index cards?

Functions

Set 1: Real-World Situation Graphs

Goal: To provide opportunities for students to develop concepts and skills related to creating and interpreting graphs representing real-world situations

Common Core Standards

Functions

Use functions to model relationships between quantities.

> **8.F.5.** Describe qualitatively the functional relationship between two quantities by analyzing a graph (e.g., where the function is increasing or decreasing, linear or nonlinear). Sketch a graph that exhibits the qualitative features of a function that has been described verbally.

Student Activities Overview and Answer Key

Station 1

Students will be given a ruler and graph paper. They work together to graph the linear equation of two cell phone company plans. Then they use the graph to compare the two cell phone plans.

Answers

1. $y = 40 + 0.5x$; answers will vary, possible values include:

Minutes (x)	5	10	20	35	45
Cost in $ (y)	42.5	45	50	57.50	62.50

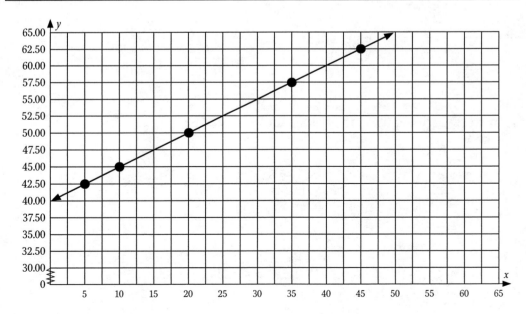

2. $y = 60 + 0.1x$; answers will vary, possible values include:

Minutes (x)	5	10	20	35	45
Cost in $ (y)	60.50	61	62	63.50	64.50

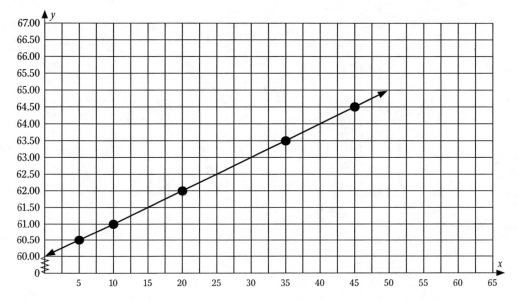

3. They should choose Bell Phone's plan because it only costs $55 versus $63.

4. They should choose Ring Phone's plan because it only costs $68 versus $80.

5. At 50 minutes, it doesn't matter which plan the customer chose because both plans cost $65.

Station 2

Students will be given a ruler and graph paper. They will work together to complete a table of values given an equation, and then graph the equation. They will analyze the slope of the graph as it applies to a real-world value.

Answers

1. $y = 20x + 10$

2. Answers will vary. Possible table of values:

Number of months	Account balance ($)
0	10
2	50
4	90
5	110
8	170
9	190

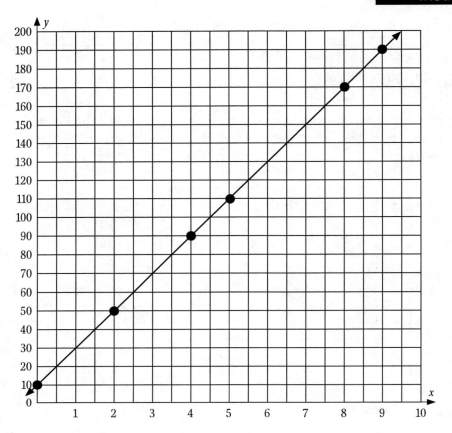

3. He will have $310 in his savings account after 15 months. This will allow him to buy the $300 stereo.

4. The slope of the graph would be steeper because the amount he saves each month represents the slope.

5. The slope of the graph would not be as steep because the amount he saves each month represents the slope.

Station 3

Students will be given a real-world graph of calories burned per mile for runners. They will interpret the graph and explain how to find an equation from the graph.

Answers

1. 60 calories per mile

2. about 69 calories per mile

3. about 81 calories per mile

4. 125 pounds

5. 150 pounds

6. Use two points to find the slope. Use a point and point-slope form to find the equation of the graph.

Station 4

Students will be given a graph that represents the temperature change in the United States in January from 1999–2009. They will analyze the temperature increase and decrease and how it relates to slope.

Answers

1. 2005–06

2. It had the steepest positive slope.

3. 2006–07

4. It had the steepest negative slope.

5. 1999–2000, 2000–01, 2002–03, 2003–04, 2006–07, 2007–08

6. 2001–02, 2004–05, 2005–06, 2008–09

Materials List/Setup

Station 1   graph paper; ruler

Station 2   graph paper; ruler

Station 3   none

Station 4   calculator

Discussion Guide

To support students in reflecting on the activities and to gather some formative information about student learning, use the following prompts to facilitate a class discussion to "debrief" the station activities.

Prompts/Questions

1. Using a graph, how can you find the x-value given its y-value?

2. Using a graph, how can you find the y-value given its x-value?

3. Using a graph, how can you find the x- and y-intercepts of the graph?

4. How can you use an equation to plot its graph?

5. What are examples of real-world situations in which you could construct a graph to represent the data?

6. Do graphs of most real-world situations represent a linear equation? Why or why not?

Think, Pair, Share

Have students jot down their own responses to questions, then discuss with a partner (who was not in their station group), and then discuss as a whole class.

Suggested Appropriate Responses

1. On the graph, move your finger across from the y-axis to the line. Move your finger down to the x-axis to find the x-value.

2. On the graph, move your finger from the x-axis up to the line. Move your finger straight across to the y-axis to find the y-value.

3. The x-intercept is where the graph crosses the x-axis. The y-intercept is where the graph crosses the y-axis.

4. Create a table of values that are solutions to the equation. Graph these ordered pairs and draw a line through these points.

5. Answers will vary. Possible answers: Business: yearly revenues; Biology: growth rate; Finance: savings account balance

6. No. Linear equations have a consistent slope. In the real world, the rate of increase or decrease is often variable because of many outside factors.

Possible Misunderstandings/Mistakes

- Reversing the x-values and the y-values when reading the graph
- Incorrectly reading the graph by matching up the wrong x- and y-values
- Reversing the x-values and y-values when constructing the graph
- Incorrectly plugging x-values into the given equation to find the y-values

Functions
Set 1: Real-World Situation Graphs

Station 1

You will be given a ruler and graph paper. Work together to analyze data from the real-world situation described below, then, as a group, answer the questions.

> You are going to get a new cell phone and need to choose between two cell phone companies. Bell Phone Company charges $40 per month. It costs $0.50 per minute after you have gone over the monthly number of minutes included in the plan. Ring Phone Company charges $60 per month. It costs $0.10 per minute after you go over the monthly number of minutes included in the plan.

Let x = minutes used that exceeded the plan. Let y = cost of the plan.

1. Write an equation that represents the cost of the Bell Phone Company's plan.

   _____

   Complete the table by selecting values for x and calculating y.

Minutes (x)					
Cost in $ (y)					

Use your graph paper to graph the ordered pairs. Use your ruler to draw a straight line through the points and complete the graph.

2. Write an equation that represents the cost of Ring Phone Company's plan.

   _____

   Complete the table selecting values for x and calculating y.

Minutes (x)					
Cost in $ (y)					

continued

Functions

Set 1: Real-World Situation Graphs

On the same graph, plot the ordered pairs. Use your ruler to draw a straight line through the points and complete the graph. Use your graphs to answer the following questions.

3. Which plan should a customer choose if he or she uses 30 minutes of extra time each month? Explain.

4. Which plan should a customer choose if he or she uses 80 minutes of extra time each month? Explain.

5. At what number of extra minutes per month would it not matter which phone plan the customer chose since the cost would be the same? Explain.

Functions
Set 1: Real-World Situation Graphs

Station 2

You will be given a ruler and graph paper. Use the information from the problem scenario below to answer the questions. Let x = months and y = savings account balance.

Marcus is going to start saving $20 every month to buy a stereo. His parents gave him $10 for his birthday to open his savings account.

1. Write an equation that represents Marcus's savings account balance x months after he began saving.

    _____

2. Complete the table by selecting variables for x and calculating y.

Number of months	Account balance ($)

Use your graph paper to define the scale of the x- and y-axes and graph the ordered pairs. Use your ruler to draw a straight line through the points and complete the graph.

3. Use your graph to estimate the number of months it will take Marcus to save enough money for a $300 stereo. Explain.

continued

Functions

Set 1: Real-World Situation Graphs

4. If Marcus saved $40 per month instead of $20, how would you expect the slope of the graph to change? Explain.

5. If Marcus saved $10 per month instead of $20, how would you expect the slope of the graph to change? Explain.

Functions
Set 1: Real-World Situation Graphs

Station 3

The equation $y = 0.6x$ represents the number of calories (y) that a runner burns per mile based on their body weight of x pounds.

For each weight below, use the graph to find the number of calories burned per mile.

1. 100 pounds: _____

2. 115 pounds: _____

3. 135 pounds: _____

For each amount of calories burned per mile below, use the graph to find the matching weight of the person.

4. 75 calories burned: _____

5. 90 calories burned: _____

6. If you didn't know the equation of this graph, how could you use the graph to find the equation of the line? Explain.

Functions
Set 1: Real-World Situation Graphs

Station 4

NOAA Satellite and Information Service created the graph below, which depicts the U.S. National Summary of the temperature in January from 1999–2009.

National Summary of January Temperatures
1999–2009

Source: www7.ncdc.noaa.gov/CDO/CDODivisionalSelect.jsp#

1. Between which consecutive years did the United States see the greatest increase in average temperature change in January?

2. What strategy did you use to answer problem 1?

continued

Functions
Set 1: Real-World Situation Graphs

3. Between which consecutive years did the United States see the greatest decrease in average temperature change in January?

4. What strategy did you use to answer problem 3?

5. Between which consecutive years was the temperature change represented as a negative slope? Explain.

6. Between which consecutive years was the temperature change represented as a positive slope? Explain.

Functions

Set 2: Relation vs. Function and Linear vs. Nonlinear

Goal: To provide opportunities for students to develop concepts and skills related to recognizing the differences between linear and nonlinear functions and the differences between functions and relations

Common Core Standards

Functions

Define, evaluate, and compare functions.

8.F.1. Understand that a function is a rule that assigns to each input exactly one output. The graph of a function is the set of ordered pairs consisting of an input and the corresponding output.[1]

8.F.2. Compare properties of two functions each represented in a different way (algebraically, graphically, numerically in tables, or by verbal descriptions).

Student Activities Overview and Answer Key

Station 1

Students will compare two different linear functions represented in different ways. The first function is represented in a table and the second function is represented as a graph. Students will interpret the slope and y-intercepts of both functions and suggest a real world-scenario for both functions.

Answers

1. Function 2; the slope of Function 1 is 2 and the slope of Function 2 is 3; 3 > 2, therefore the rate of change in Function 1 is greater.

2. Function 1—for every positive change of 1 unit of x, the y-value increases by 2 units; Function 2—for every positive change of 1 unit of x, the y-value increases by 3 units.

3. Function 1 has the greater y-intercept. The y-intercept of Function 1 is 3, as shown in the table (when $x = 0$, $y = 3$). Function 2 has a y-intercept of 2, as shown in the graph. The graph for Function 2 crosses the y-axis at $y = 2$. Since 3 > 2 and Function 1 has a y-intercept of 3, it has the greater y-intercept.

4. $y = 2x + 3$

5. $y = 3x + 2$

6. Answers will vary. Be sure that students' scenarios have a rate of change of 2 and an initial value of 3. Sample answer: Michelle wants to expand her MP3 collection. She currently only has 3 songs on her MP3 player. She plans to download 2 new songs a day.

[1] Function notation is not required in Grade 8.

Functions

Set 2: Relation vs. Function and Linear vs. Nonlinear

7. Answers will vary. Be sure that students' scenarios have a rate of change of 3 and an initial value of 2. Sample answer: Bernard is offering his neighbors a great deal on mowing lawns. He charges an initial fee of $3 and then charges $2 per hour.

8. Answers will vary. Sample answer: I used the y-intercept as an initial value and the slope as the rate of change.

Station 2

At this station, students will build a model of pentagonal numbers and analyze the pattern.

Answers

Term	1	2	3	4	5	6	7
Dots	5	9	13	17	21	25	29
# of dots added from previous term	----	4	4	4	4	4	4

1. Yes, the relationship is linear because the difference between consecutive terms in the sequence is constant.

2. $4n + 1$, where n is the number of the term

3. The equation is linear.

4.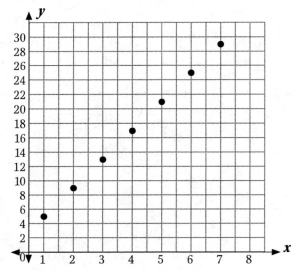

The graph is linear. The graph is a straight line.

Functions

Set 2: Relation vs. Function and Linear vs. Nonlinear

Instruction

Station 3

At this station, students will graph various equations and determine if the relations are functions by examining their graphs, tables, and mapping diagrams.

Answers

1.

x	−4	−3	−2	−1	0	1	2	3	4
y	16	9	4	1	0	1	4	9	16

2.

3.

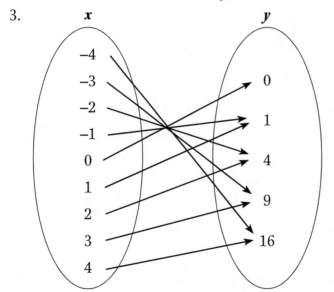

4. The relation is a function because the power on the y-variable is one in the equation. The table shows that for each x, there is only one unique y-value. In the mapping diagram, for each x, the arrow goes to only one y-value.

5.

x	16	9	4	1	0	1	4	9	16
y	−4	−3	−2	−1	0	1	2	3	4

Functions
Set 2: Relation vs. Function and Linear vs. Nonlinear

Instruction

6.

7.

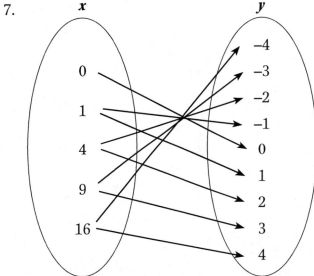

8. The relation is not a function. In the equation, the power on the *y*-variable is 2. In the table, there are, in all but one case (for 0), two values for each *x*-value. In the mapping diagram, the arrows from the *x*-values go to more than one *y*-value in all but one case (for 0).

Station 4

Students will compare two different linear functions represented in different ways. The first function is represented as an equation and the second function is represented as a verbal description. Students will compare the two functions and then create tables and graphs for both functions.

Answers

1. Both functions have a negative rate of change; both slopes are negative.

2. Function 1 has a greater *y*-intercept; $-2 > -4$

Functions
Set 2: Relation vs. Function and Linear vs. Nonlinear

Instruction

3. Tables may vary. Sample tables:

x	y
0	−2
1	−2.5
2	−3
3	−3.5
4	−4
5	−4.5

x	y
0	−4
1	−4.25
2	−4.5
3	−4.75
4	−5
5	−5.25

4. In the tables, Function 1 is decreasing by 0.5 for every positive increment of x while Function 2 is decreasing by only 0.25 for each positive increment of x; 0.5 is greater than 0.25. Additionally, when x is zero, the value of y for Function 1 is −2, while the value of y for Function 2 is −4. This shows that the y-intercept in Function 1 is greater than the y-intercept of Function 2.

5.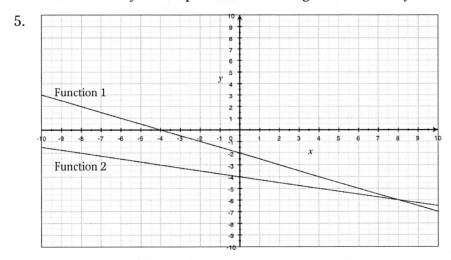

6. Answers will vary. Sample answer: The graph of Function 1 shows that it is more rapidly decreasing than Function 2. This can really be seen for values of $x > 8$. If you were to imagine placing a ball on each line, the ball would roll more quickly on Function 1's graph. Additionally, the y-intercept of Function 1 is higher on the graph than the y-intercept of Function 2, thereby showing that Function 1's y-intercept is greater.

Materials List/Setup

Station 1	none
Station 2	graph paper
Station 3	graph paper
Station 4	none

Functions
Set 2: Relation vs. Function and Linear vs. Nonlinear

Instruction

Discussion Guide

To support students in reflecting on the activities and to gather some formative information about student learning, use the following prompts to facilitate a class discussion to "debrief" the station activities.

Prompts/Questions

1. How can you compare two functions that are represented differently?

2. What determines if a relation is a function?

3. Describe the graph of any function in terms of inputs and outputs.

4. How do you determine the greater rate of change between two functions that have negative slope?

Think, Pair, Share

Have students jot down their own responses to questions, then discuss with a partner (who was not in their station group), and then discuss as a whole class.

Suggested Appropriate Responses

1. If two functions are represented differently you could convert the representation of one function into the same type of representation as the other function.

2. A relation is a function if each input gives one and only one output. On a graph, a function passes the vertical line test—if you placed an imaginary vertical line across the function, the line would only touch one point at a time on the function. In a table, the *x*-coordinate would only have one distinct *y*-coordinate. In an equation, the power of *y* would be 1 or it would otherwise have a restricted domain.

3. The graph of a function will pass the vertical line test, such that if you place an imaginary vertical line across the function, the line will only touch one point at a time on the function. This means that for each input there is exactly one distinct output.

4. When comparing negative slopes, examine the absolute value of the slopes to determine the greater rate of change.

Possible Misunderstandings/Mistakes

- Not understanding or recalling the definition of a function

- Incorrectly comparing negative slopes by forgetting to compare the absolute values of the negative slopes

- Incorrectly identifying the slope and/or *y*-intercept

Functions
Set 2: Relation vs. Function and Linear vs. Nonlinear

Station 1

There are two functions given below. Analyze each function and answer the questions that follow.

Function 1:

x	0	3	5	6	8
y	3	9	13	15	19

Function 2:

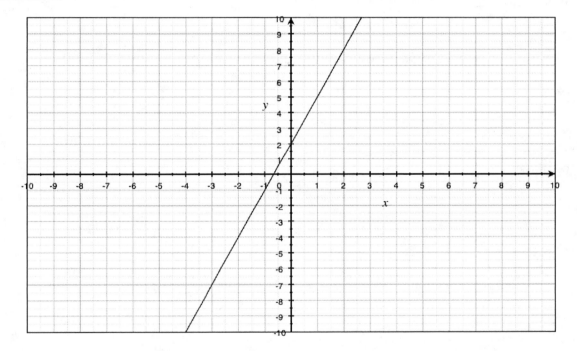

1. Which function has the greater rate of change? _____

   How do you know?

2. Describe in words the rate of change for each function.

   Function 1: _____

   Function 2: _____

continued

NAME: _____

Functions

Set 2: Relation vs. Function and Linear vs. Nonlinear

3. Which function has the greater y-intercept? _____

   How do you know?

4. What is the algebraic equation for Function 1? _____

5. What is the algebraic equation for Function 2? _____

6. Propose a real-world scenario for Function 1.

7. Propose a real-world scenario for Function 2.

8. What strategies did you use to propose your real-world scenarios?

Functions
Set 2: Relation vs. Function and Linear vs. Nonlinear

Station 2

At this station, you will extend an arithmetic sequence. The first three numbers in the sequence have been filled in for you. Continue the pattern to the 7th term. Graph the seven numbers and look for a pattern.

Term	1	2	3	4	5	6	7
Dots	5	9	13				
# of dots added from previous term	—	4					

1. Is the relationship linear? Explain your reasoning.

2. Write an algebraic equation for the nth term in the sequence. _____

3. Is the equation linear? Explain your reasoning.

4. Graph the first 7 terms of your sequence on graph paper. Describe the shape of your graph. Is your graph linear?

Functions

Set 2: Relation vs. Function and Linear vs. Nonlinear

Station 3

At this station, you will graph various equations and determine if the relations are functions by examining their graphs, points, tables, and mapping diagrams.

Given: $y = x^2$

1. Complete the table below and show your work on a separate sheet of paper if necessary.

x	−4	−3	−2	−1	0	1	2	3	4
y									

2. Use the values from your table and graph the relation on graph paper.

3. Create a mapping diagram of points from the table above.

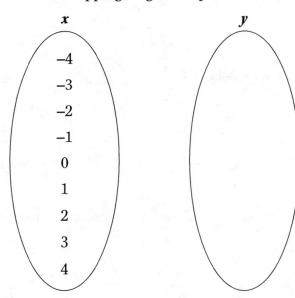

4. Is the relation a function? Use the equation, table, and mapping diagram to explain your reasoning.

continued

Functions

Set 2: Relation vs. Function and Linear vs. Nonlinear

Use the information below to complete 5–8.

Given: $y^2 = x$

5. Complete the table below and show your work on a separate sheet of paper if necessary.

x									
y	−4	−3	−2	−1	0	1	2	3	4

6. Use the values from your table and graph the relation on graph paper.

7. Create a mapping diagram of points from the table above.

 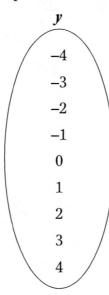

x   y
−4
−3
−2
−1
0
1
2
3
4

8. Is the relation a function? Use the equation, table, and mapping diagram to explain your reasoning.

Functions
Set 2: Relation vs. Function and Linear vs. Nonlinear

Station 4

Analyze the equation and the scenario given below. Use these to answer the questions that follow.

Function 1: $y = -\dfrac{1}{2}x - 2$

Function 2: Omar owes his mother $4. She tells him that for each day he does not pay her back she is going to charge him 25 cents.

1. Which function(s) have a negative rate of change? _____

    Explain your thinking.

2. Which function has the greater y-intercept? _____

    Explain your thinking.

3. Create tables for Functions 1 and 2 below.

    Function 1

x	y

    Function 2

x	y

4. How do the tables for Function 1 and Function 2 support your answers to questions 1 and 2?

continued

Functions

Set 2: Relation vs. Function and Linear vs. Nonlinear

5. Graph both functions on the same coordinate plane.

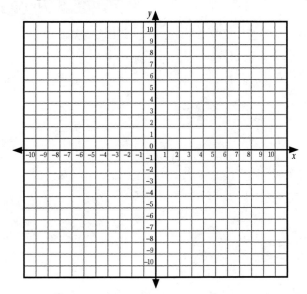

6. How do the graphs support your answers to questions 1 and 2?

Functions

Set 3: Slope and Slope-Intercept Form

Goal: To provide opportunities for students to develop concepts and skills related to coordinate graphing

Common Core Standards

Functions

Define, evaluate, and compare functions.

8.F.3. Interpret the equation $y = mx + b$ as defining a linear function, whose graph is a straight line; give examples of functions that are not linear.

Student Activities Overview and Answer Key

Station 1

Students work together to complete a table for the linear equation $y = 4x - 3$. They use the completed table to plot points and draw the graph of the equation. Then they name other points that lie on the line and describe the relationship between the x- and y-values of these points.

Answers

1.

x	y
−3	−15
−1	−7
0	−3
2	5
3	9

2–4.

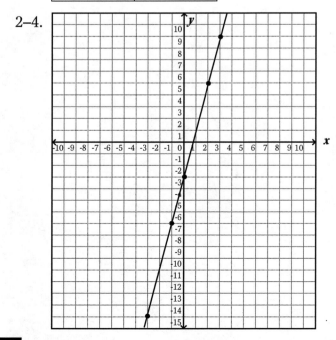

Functions

Set 3: Slope and Slope-Intercept Form

5. Possible answer: $(-2, -11)$, $(1, 1)$, $(4, 13)$

6. The x- and y-values are related by the equation $y = 4x - 3$.

Station 2

In this activity, students are given a table of values. They work together to plot these points and look for patterns. (The points all satisfy the relationship $y = -x + 5$, so they all lie on a straight line.) Using the graph of plotted points, students name additional points that they think satisfy the same relationship. Then they describe this relationship by writing an equation.

Answers

1–2.

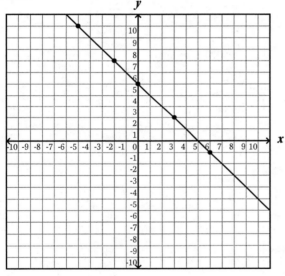

3. The points all lie on a straight line

4. Possible answer: $(-4, 9)$, $(1, 4)$, and $(7, -2)$

5. $y = -x + 5$; The y-value is always 5 more than the opposite of the x-value.

Functions

Set 3: Slope and Slope-Intercept Form

Station 3

Students work together to explore a pattern made from tiles. They complete a table showing the relationship between the stage of the pattern and the number of tiles needed. Then they plot the points (which lie on the line $y = 3x - 1$) and use the graph to predict the number of tiles that would be needed to make Stage 7 of the pattern. Then they express the relationship by writing an equation.

Answers

1.

Stage (x)	1	2	3	4	5
Number of tiles (y)	2	5	8	11	14

2–3.

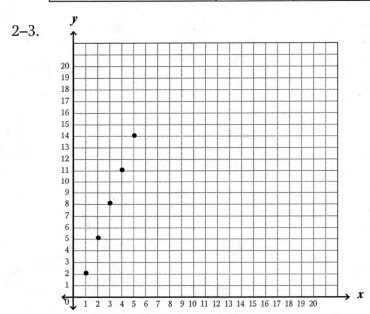

4. 20 tiles

5. $y = 3x - 1$; The number of tiles is always 3 times the number of the stage minus 1.

Station 4

Students work together to explore and graph a linear equation based on a real-world situation. First students complete a table of values that show the temperature of a freezer at various times. Then they work together to plot the points and draw the linear graph. They use their graph to estimate the number of hours it takes for the temperature of the freezer to reach 0°F.

Functions

Set 3: Slope and Slope-Intercept Form

Answers

1.

Hour (*x*)	0	1	4	5	7
Temperature, °F (*y*)	15	11	−1	−5	−13

2–4.

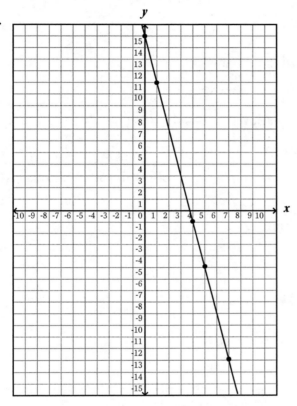

5. Possible estimate: 3.5 hours (actual answer is 3.75 hours)

6. Estimate the *x*-value where the graph of the line crosses the *x*-axis.

Materials List/Setup

Station 1   graph paper; ruler

Station 2   graph paper; ruler

Station 3   small square tiles; graph paper; ruler

Station 4   graph paper; ruler

Discussion Guide

To support students in reflecting on the activities and to gather some formative information about student learning, use the following prompts to facilitate a class discussion to "debrief" the station activities.

Prompts/Questions

1. How do you plot an ordered pair on a coordinate plane?

2. What steps do you use to graph an equation on a coordinate plane?

3. What can you say about the graph of any equation that has the form $y = mx + b$?

4. If you are given the graph of a line, how can you find the equation of the line?

5. Which method (table, intercepts, slope-intercept form) of graphing linear equations is the easiest and why?

6. Which method is easiest to use for determining the slope?

Think, Pair, Share

Have students jot down their own responses to questions, then discuss with a partner (who was not in their station group), and then discuss as a whole class.

Suggested Appropriate Responses

1. First plot the *x*-value by moving along the *x*-axis by the given number of units (right if the *x*-value is positive, left if it is negative). Then move up or down from this point to plot the *y*-value (up if the *y*-value is positive, down if it is negative).

2. Use the equation to make a table of *x*- and *y*-values. Use the table to form ordered pairs. Plot these points. Draw a line or curve through the points to complete the graph.

3. The graph of the equation is a straight line.

4. Find several points on the line. Look for a relationship between the *x*-values and the *y*-values. Write a rule (equation) that relates the *x*-values and *y*-values.

5. Answers will vary. Sample answers:

    Graphing using a table will always work if you forget the shortcut methods of intercepts and slope-intercept. The intercepts method is fast if the coefficients are factors of the constant. Slope-intercept form is easiest when the *x*- and *y*-intercepts are fractions.

6. If the equation is already in slope-intercept form, the slope is easy to determine because no calculations or graphing are necessary.

Possible Misunderstandings/Mistakes

- Incorrectly plotting points due to reversing the *x*- and *y*-values (e.g., plotting (3, 4) rather than (4, 3))

- Incorrectly plotting points due to mislabeling or incorrectly calibrating the scale on the *x*- or *y*-axis

- Incorrectly reading the ordered pairs from a table of values

Functions
Set 3: Slope and Slope-Intercept Form

Station 1

At this station, you will work together to make a table and graph for the following equation:

$y = 4x - 3$

x	y
–3	
–1	
0	
2	
3	

1. Work with other students to complete the table of values.

2. Set up a coordinate plane on a sheet of graph paper. Use a ruler to draw the x-axis and the y-axis.

3. Plot the ordered pairs from your table. Work together to make sure that all the points are plotted correctly.

4. Use the points to draw the complete graph of the equation $y = 4x - 3$.

5. Name at least three points that lie on the graph aside from the ones you plotted.

6. What do you know about the x- and y-values of these points?

Functions
Set 3: Slope and Slope-Intercept Form

Station 2

At this station, you will plot points from a table and use your graph to write an equation.

The table shows a set of values. Work with other students to explore how the *x*- and *y*-values are related.

x	y
−5	10
−2	7
0	5
3	2
6	−1

1. Set up a coordinate plane on a sheet of graph paper. Use a ruler to draw the *x*-axis and the *y*-axis.

2. Plot the ordered pairs. Work together to make sure that all the points are plotted correctly.

3. Describe what you notice about the points.

4. Use your graph to help you name at least three additional points that you think have the same relationship between their *x*-value and their *y*-value.

5. What is the equation that relates the *x*-values and *y*-values? Explain.

Functions
Set 3: Slope and Slope-Intercept Form

Station 3

At this station, you will use a table and graph to explore a pattern. You can also use tiles to build the pattern. Work with other students to explore the pattern.

Sonia is using tiles to make a pattern for a patio in her garden. Here are the first three stages in her pattern.

1. Complete the table.

Stage (x)	1	2	3	4	5
Number of tiles (y)					

2. Set up a coordinate plane on a sheet of graph paper. Use a ruler to draw the x-axis and the y-axis.

3. Plot the ordered pairs. Work together to make sure that all the points are plotted correctly.

4. Use your graph to predict the number of tiles that are needed at Stage 7. _____

5. Write an equation that gives the number of tiles y for any given stage x. Explain how you found the equation.

NAME: _____

Functions
Set 3: Slope and Slope-Intercept Form

Station 4

Work together to analyze a table of data from a real-world situation.

A scientist is doing an experiment with bacteria in a freezer. The equation $y = 15 - 4x$ gives the temperature y of the freezer x hours after the start of the experiment.

1. Complete the table.

Hour (x)	0	1	4	5	7
Temperature, °F (y)					

2. Set up a coordinate plane on a sheet of graph paper. Use a ruler to draw the x-axis and the y-axis.

3. Plot the ordered pairs. Work together to make sure that all the points are plotted correctly.

4. Use the points you plotted to draw the complete graph of $y = 15 - 4x$.

5. Use your graph to estimate the number of hours it takes for the freezer to reach 0°F.

   _____

6. Explain how you made this estimate.

Geometry

Goal: To provide opportunities for students to develop concepts and skills related to
understanding transformations

Common Core Standards

Geometry

Understand congruence and similarity using physical models, transparencies, or geometry software.

8.G.1. Verify experimentally the properties of rotations, reflections, and translations:

a. Lines are taken to lines, and line segments to line segments of the same length.

b. Angles are taken to angles of the same measure.

c. Parallel lines are taken to parallel lines.

8.G.3. Describe the effect of dilations, translations, rotations, and reflections on two-dimensional figures using coordinates.

Student Activities Overview and Answer Key

Station 1

Students will draw a figure on the coordinate plane. They will then perform a variety of transformations, keeping track of the new coordinates along the way. They use the knowledge they gained to predict the new coordinates of another figure that underwent a transformation.

Answers: Answers will vary; answers will vary; answers will vary; (–2, 1), (–1, 7) and (1, 3)—you need to subtract 3 from the x-coordinate

Station 2

At this station, students practice translations by leading a dot through a maze. Then need to explain each translation and give the new coordinates. They then describe their strategies.

Answers: New coordinates—(1, –5), (6, –5), (6, –9), (2, –9), (2, –14), (11, –14), (11, –10), (14, –10); answers will vary

Station 3

Students draw a figure on the coordinate plane. They then perform dilations and draw how that affects their figures. They also state the coordinates of their new figures.

Answers: Answers may vary; answers may vary; answers may vary; you multiply the coordinates by whatever the dilation factor is

Station 4

At this station, students look at reflection. They reflect two images and then have the opportunity to create their own. Finally, they reflect on an effective strategy for finding the coordinates of a reflection.

Answers: Answers will vary—possibly counting away from the y-axis

Materials List/Setup

Station 1   enough rulers for all group members

Station 2   none

Station 3   none

Station 4   none

Discussion Guide

To support students in reflecting on the activities and to gather some formative information about student learning, use the following prompts to facilitate a class discussion to "debrief" the station activities.

Prompts/Questions

1. What is an example of a real-life situation where we use dilations?

2. How does a reflection over the x-axis affect the coordinates of a figure?

3. What is an example of a reflection in real-life?

4. Is a translation more like doing the Electric Slide or being on a merry-go-round? Explain.

Think, Pair, Share

Have students jot down their own responses to questions, then discuss with a partner (who was not in their station group), and then discuss as a whole class.

Suggested Appropriate Responses

1. many possibilities—pictures

2. It changes the sign of the y-coordinates

3. many possibilities—the right and left hand

4. Electric Slide—slide is in the name

Possible Misunderstandings/Mistakes

- Reflecting over the wrong line

- Confusing dilation—only changing one coordinate or dividing instead of multiplying by the factor of dilation

- Having trouble with negative coordinates

Geometry
Set 1: Transformations

Station 1

At this station, you will be performing various transformations. As a group, agree on what you'll do.

In the coordinate plane below, draw a simple figure. Try to go through points when possible. You must pass through at least five whole number points and label them on your graph (for example, (3, 1), and so on).

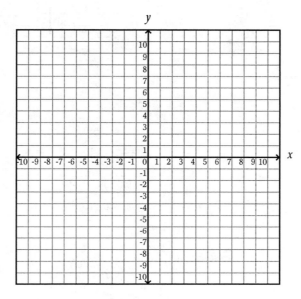

Reflect your figure over the *y*-axis.

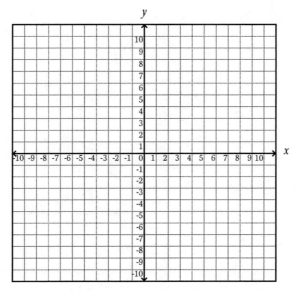

What are the new coordinates? Did everyone come up with the same coordinates? Why or why not?

continued

Now move your figure down three.

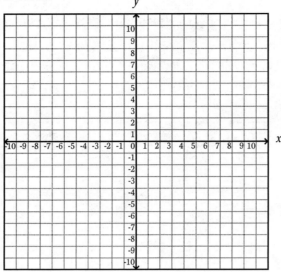

What are the new coordinates? Did everyone get the same coordinates? Why or why not?

Finally, rotate your figure 180 degrees.

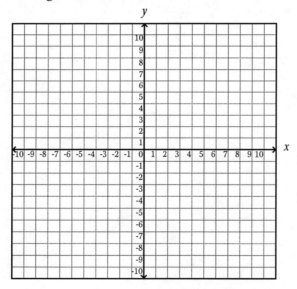

What are the new coordinates? Did everyone get the same coordinates? Why or why not?

If there was a triangle with coordinates of (1, 1), (2, 7) and (4, 3), and you wanted to shift it three units to the left, what would the new coordinates be? Explain how you arrived at your answer.

Geometry
Set 1: Transformations

Station 2

At this station, you will lead a dot through a maze by explaining the necessary translations (e.g., slides, flips).

Below is a maze. Imagine a dot at the beginning. Your group's goal is to get to the bottom right where there is a break in the graph. Imagine that the top left corner is (0, 0).

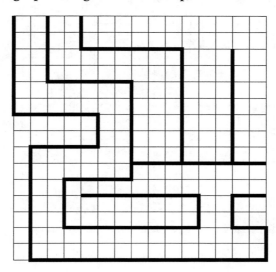

Discuss the steps. In the table below, list the translation in words and the coordinates of the new point where the dot will be after each move.

Turn	Translation in words	New coordinates
1		
2		
3		
4		
5		
6		
7		
8		

What were your strategies for going through this maze? _____

_____

_____

Geometry

Set 1: Transformations

Station 3

Discuss as a group, and agree on a simple figure to draw on the coordinate plane below. It needs to intersect at least five whole number pairs of coordinates.

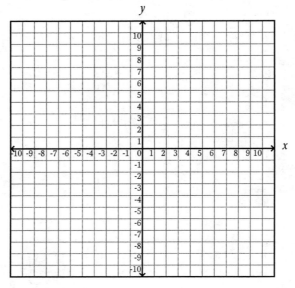

What are your coordinates? _____

Dilate your figure by a factor of two.

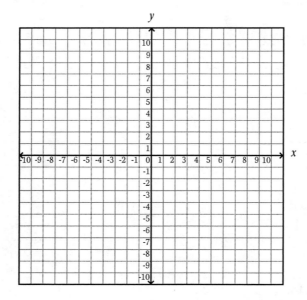

continued

Geometry
Set 1: Transformations

Discuss with your group. What are your new coordinates? Does everyone agree? Why or why not?

_____

_____

_____

Dilate your original figure by a factor of $\frac{1}{2}$.

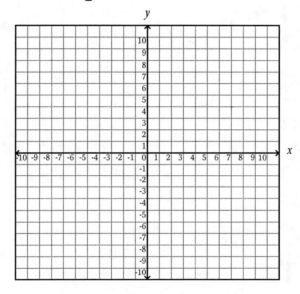

Discuss with your group. What are your new coordinates? Does everyone agree? Why or why not?

_____

_____

_____

How does dilation affect the coordinates? _____

_____

_____

Geometry
Set 1: Transformations

Station 4

At this station, you will find a ruler. You will use this to create various reflections.

Look at the two figures below. Draw a reflection across the *y*-axis.

   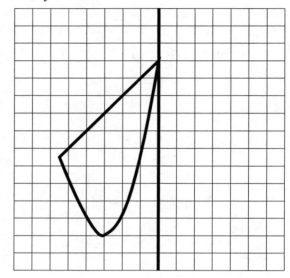

Create a drawing on the grid below. Also draw the reflection.

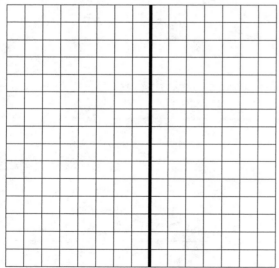

What was your strategy for finding the reflections? Do all your reflections look the same? Why or why not?

_____

_____

Geometry

Set 2: Translations and Rotations

Goal: To provide opportunities for students to develop concepts and skills related to translations and rotations of plane figures through space

Common Core Standards

Geometry

Understand congruence and similarity using physical models, transparencies, or geometry software.

8.G.1. Verify experimentally the properties of rotations, reflections, and translations:

    a. Lines are taken to lines, and line segments to line segments of the same length.

    b. Angles are taken to angles of the same measure.

    c. Parallel lines are taken to parallel lines.

8.G.2. Understand that a two-dimensional figure is congruent to another if the second can be obtained from the first by a sequence of rotations, reflections, and translations; given two congruent figures, describe a sequence that exhibits the congruence between them.

8.G.3. Describe the effect of dilations, translations, rotations, and reflections on two-dimensional figures using coordinates.

Student Activities Overview and Answer Key

Station 1

Students construct rectangles and tape them around a pencil to see how rotating a rectangle forms a cylinder. They then reflect on what part of the rectangle formed the parts of the cylinder.

Answers: a cylinder; the width of the rectangle; a cylinder

Station 2

Students examine a penny and then spin it. They look at what solid the penny looks like when it spins. They then reflect on their experience and apply this to new shapes.

Answers: a circle; a sphere; yes; rotate it around a point on the side of the penny

Station 3

Students explore what happens when a square is translated through space. They first imagine what shape would form, and then place tiles back to back to form the figure. Finally, they apply what they have learned to answer a related question.

Answers: Answers will vary; a rectangular prism; you'd need to know the height or by how many units you were translating the square

Station 4

Students explore how they would turn a circle into a cylinder through translation. They also discuss the volume of the figure they create through either a translation or rotation in space.

Answers: Answers will vary; a translation through space; we just have to multiply the area of the circle by the height of the cylinder to get the volume; answers will vary; no, and the volume would change

Materials List/Setup

Station 1	enough scrap paper and scissors for all group members; tape and a pencil
Station 2	enough pennies for all group members
Station 3	15 one-inch square tiles
Station 4	a paper towel roll

Discussion Guide

To support students in reflecting on the activities and to gather some formative information about student learning, use the following prompts to facilitate a class discussion to "debrief" the station activities.

Prompts/Questions

1. What is the difference between translating a circle through space and rotating a circle in space?

2. What solid would you get if you rotated a triangle in space?

3. When do we rotate solids in real life?

4. What solid would you get if you translated a triangle in space?

Think, Pair, Share

Have students jot down their own responses to questions, then discuss with a partner (who was not in their station group), and then discuss as a whole class.

Suggested Appropriate Responses

1. translation—cylinder; rotation—sphere

2. a cone

3. There are many examples, such as when using a pottery wheel.

4. a triangular prism

Possible Misunderstandings/Mistakes

- Having trouble visualizing plane figures moving through space
- Not correctly taping the paper to the pencil
- Believing that you must always rotate around a figure's center

Geometry
Set 2: Translations and Rotations

Station 1

At this station, you will find enough scrap paper and scissors for all group members. You will also find tape and a pencil.

Decide on the dimensions of a rectangle that you would like to use for this task. Each group member should cut out several rectangles of the same size. Tape each rectangle to the pencil so that one side of the rectangle (the length side) is touching the pencil.

Repeat this process at different points around the pencil until all the rectangles are attached.

What solid have you formed? (Look at the pencil from all sides and imagine that there were many more rectangles taped to it.)

_____

In this case, the radius of your solid is equal to what part of the rectangle? _____

If you have a rectangle and spin it, what solid does it form? _____

Geometry
Set 2: Translations and Rotations

Station 2

At this station, you will find enough pennies for all members of your group.

What shape is a penny? _____

Spin your penny. Look at it as it spins. Does it look like it turns into a three-dimensional shape? What shape?

_____

Do you think the radius of the penny is the same as the radius of the three-dimensional shape you seem to see?

_____

Discuss with your group. How would you rotate a penny through space to get a ring or doughnut? Explain.

_____

_____

_____

_____

Geometry
Set 2: Translations and Rotations

Station 3

At this station, you will find 1-inch square tiles. Work with your group to learn about translating squares in space.

Take one of the squares and move it along the table with one of the sides (not the face) touching the table.

Describe the figure a square makes when it is translated in this manner.

_____

Now place ten of the squares so their faces are touching and they are standing on one of their sides. What figure did you make?

_____

Describe how you could find the volume of a rectangular prism by translating a square through space.

_____

_____

_____

Geometry
Set 2: Translations and Rotations

Station 4

At this station, you will find a paper towel roll. Trace an end of the paper towel roll on the grid below.

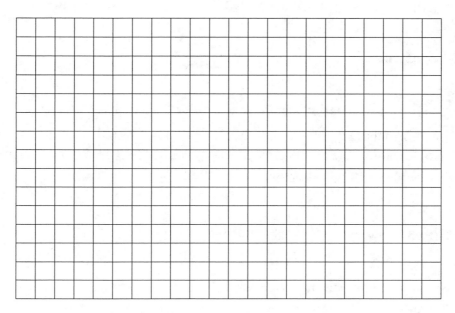

Discuss with your group and answer the questions below.

What is the area of this circle? _____

What could be done to this circle to form a cylinder (e.g., translation, rotation, etc.)?

_____

_____

How is knowing the area of the circle the first step to finding the volume of a cylinder?

_____

_____

What is the volume of the cylinder? _____

If you spun the circle through space, would you still get a cylinder? Would the volume be the same?

_____

Geometry

Goal: To provide opportunities for students to develop concepts and skills related to applying
properties of angle pairs formed by parallel lines cut by a transversal

Common Core Standards

Geometry

Understand congruence and similarity using physical models, transparencies, or geometry software.

8.G.5. Use informal arguments to establish facts about the angle sum and exterior angle of
triangles, about the angles created when parallel lines are cut by a transversal, and the
angle-angle criterion for similarity of triangles.

Student Activities Overview and Answer Key

Station 1

Students draw two parallel lines cut by a transversal. They then measure the resulting angles and
draw conclusions about their observations.

Answers: *D, E, H; C, F, G;* many answers, (e.g., *A* and *F*)

Station 2

Students use a geoboard to construct parallel lines cut by a transversal. They then measure the
resulting angles and draw conclusions about their observations.

Answers: Parallel lines cut by transversals form congruent and supplementary angles; 2; many
possibilities—2 sets of 4 congruent angles

Station 3

Students find parallel lines cut by a transversal around the room. They measure the angles formed
and draw conclusions based on their observations.

Answers: Answers will vary—there are only two unique angles; two

Station 4

Students work backwards to construct parallel lines. They begin with a line and construct two lines that intersect that line at the same angle. They then discover that they have constructed parallel lines.

Answers: The distance between the lines is always the same; yes; they are equidistant at all points

Materials List/Setup

Station 1	ruler, pencil, and protractor for each group member
Station 2	geoboard, rubber bands, and a protractor
Station 3	ruler; protractor
Station 4	ruler and protractor for each group member

Discussion Guide

To support students in reflecting on the activities and to gather some formative information about student learning, use the following prompts to facilitate a class discussion to "debrief" the station activities.

Prompts/Questions

1. What is a real-life example of when you would find two parallel lines cut by a transversal?

2. When would it be important to know that vertical angles are congruent?

3. What is a strategy for proving that two lines are parallel?

4. How are geoboards helpful when working with parallel lines and transversals?

Think, Pair, Share

Have students jot down their own responses to questions, then discuss with a partner (who was not in their station group), and then discuss as a whole class.

Suggested Appropriate Responses

1. Many possibilities—top and bottom of a wall and the door frame, window frames

2. Many possibilities—design and construction

3. see if they have the same angle off of the transversal

4. The pegs are parallel, which can help construct the desired situation.

Possible Misunderstandings/Mistakes

* Having trouble measuring the angles of things around the room that are not flat

* Not properly measuring the distance between two lines which could alter results and the observations

* Mislabeling diagrams

Geometry
Set 3: Properties of Angle Pairs

Station 1

At this station, you will be discovering relationships between angles that are formed when a set of parallel lines is cut by a transversal. You will find pencils, rulers, and protractors to help you with this task. Work with your group to complete the activities.

Below is a set of parallel lines. Using your ruler, draw a transversal—a line that goes through both of the parallel lines.

The top angle on the left should be named *A*, the top angle on the right should be named *B*, and so forth. It should look like the example below (but the line cutting the parallel lines can cut them at any angle).

```
    A │ B
 ──────────
    C │ D

    E │ F
 ──────────
    G │ H
```

Measure your angles and record them in the table below.

Angle	Measure in degrees	Angle	Measure in degrees
A		*E*	
B		*F*	
C		*G*	
D		*H*	

What angles are congruent to *A*? _____

What angles are congruent to *B*? _____

Name a pair of supplementary angles that are not touching. _____

Geometry
Set 3: Properties of Angle Pairs

Station 2

At this station, you will find a geoboard, rubber bands, and protractors. Work with your group to complete the activities.

Using the geoboard, construct a set of parallel lines. Use another rubber band to make a transversal. Measure the angles formed from the parallel lines and the transversal. Draw the situation below, labeling the angles.

Repeat this step again using a different transversal.

What are your observations?

_____

_____

How many different angle measurements did you get for each geoboard? _____

Finish the following sentence.

Two parallel lines cut by a transversal form _____

_____

Geometry
Set 3: Properties of Angle Pairs

Station 3

In this activity, your group will be locating parallel lines cut by transversals around the room. You will have a protractor and ruler with you to help.

As a group, find three examples of parallel lines cut by a transversal in the room (e.g., a pen lying on lined paper).

Measure the eight angles formed in each example. Record this information in the table below.

Example	Measure of angle

What do you notice about the measure of the angles?

_____

_____

_____

How many unique angles are created when two parallel lines are cut by a transversal?

_____

Geometry
Set 3: Properties of Angle Pairs

Station 4

At this station, you will find enough rulers and protractors for everyone in the group. Each group member should complete the activity and then discuss your observations as a group.

Draw a line in the space below.

Now draw two lines coming off of the original line at the same angle.

Measure the distance between the two new lines at least five times. Record that data below.

Distance between two lines

What do you notice? _____

_____

_____

Are the two lines parallel? _____

How do you know? _____

_____

_____

Geometry

Set 4: Properties of Lines Cut by Transversals

Goal: To provide opportunities for students to develop concepts and skills related to understanding the properties of the ratio of segments of parallel lines that have been cut by one or more transversals

Common Core Standards

Geometry

Understand congruence and similarity using physical models, transparencies, or geometry software.

8.G.5. Use informal arguments to establish facts about the angle sum and exterior angle of triangles, about the angles created when parallel lines are cut by a transversal, and the angle-angle criterion for similarity of triangles.

Student Activities Overview and Answer Key

Station 1

Students draw transversals through three parallel lines and then measure the segments that are between the lines. Then they calculate the ratio of these segments and draw conclusions.

Answers: The ratios are the same; similar observations about ratios; the ratio is the same

Station 2

Students draw a triangle using a base that is parallel to another segment. Then they compare the ratios of various line segments in the triangle. In the end, they apply what they know about similar triangles to explain the observations they made about the ratios.

Answers: Answers will vary; answers will vary; answers will vary; answers will vary; answers will vary; answers will vary; the ratios are the same; triangles *DCE* and *ACB* are similar triangles so their sides are proportional

Station 3

Students draw a segment through a trapezoid and make sure it is parallel to the base. Then they measure the new pieces of the trapezoid and find various ratios. They conclude by making a general statement about what happens when a trapezoid is cut by a parallel line.

Answers: Answers will vary; answers will vary; answers will vary; answers will vary; answers will vary; answers will vary; They are proportional; The segments are cut into proportional sections.

Station 4

Students explore what happens when a set of parallel lines is intersected by another pair of parallel lines. They take measurements and find ratios. Finally, students decide what type of figure is created when this happens.

Answers: Answers will vary; answers will vary; answers will vary; answers will vary; 1; 1; The ratios are both 1; a parallelogram

Materials List/Setup

All Stations   calculator and ruler for each group member

Discussion Guide

To support students in reflecting on the activities and to gather some formative information about student learning, use the following prompts to facilitate a class discussion to "debrief" the station activities.

Prompts/Questions

1. When is it important to know that there is a ratio between two lines or other objects?

2. When is it important in math to know that when parallel lines are cut by transversals they are broken into proportional pieces?

3. What types of figures are formed when you use a parallel line to cut a figure into more than one piece?

4. How are similar triangle and transversals of parallel lines related?

Think, Pair, Share

Have students jot down their own responses to questions, then discuss with a partner (who was not in their station group), and then discuss as a whole class.

Suggested Appropriate Responses

1. Many possibilities—when building something from a model or to scale

2. Many possibilities—when proving certain properties, solving problems with missing measurements

3. similar figures

4. Both have proportional sides as a result of similar angles.

Possible Misunderstandings/Mistakes

- Not accurately measuring with the ruler
- Flipping ratios
- Incorrectly labeling diagrams

Geometry
Set 4: Properties of Lines Cut by Transversals

Station 1

At this station, you will find enough calculators and rulers for all members of the group. Each group member should complete the activity and then discuss observations with the group.

Below are three parallel line segments. Draw two new segments that intersect these three segments. Label these segments 1 and 2.

———————————————————————— *a*

———————————————————————— *b*

———————————————————————— *c*

Fill in the table below using the measurements of the line segments you drew.

Line	Length *ab*	Length *bc*	*ab/bc*
1			
2			

What do you notice? _____

_____

Compare your answers with other group members. In what ways were their observations similar or different?

_____

_____

_____

What is true about the ratio of segments of transversals that have been cut by the same parallel lines?

_____

_____

Geometry
Set 4: Properties of Lines Cut by Transversals

Station 2

At this station, you will find enough rulers and calculators for all group members. Each person should complete the activity and discuss your observations with your group.

Below is a set of parallel line segments. Line segment *AB* is going to be the base of a triangle.

Draw in point *C* somewhere above line segment *k*.

Draw segments *AC* and *BC*. Label the point where *AC* intersects *k* as *D*. Label the point where *BC* intersects *k* as *E*.

k

A ●━━━━━━━━━━━━━━━━● *B*

Find the length of the following segments.

AD = _____   *DC* = _____

BE = _____   *EC* = _____

Find the following ratios.

AD/DC = _____   *BE/EC* = _____

What do you notice?

_____

_____

As a group, use your knowledge of similar triangles to explain.

_____

_____

_____

Geometry
Set 4: Properties of Lines Cut by Transversals

Station 3

At this station, you will find enough rulers and calculators for all group members. Each person should complete the activity and discuss observations with the group.

Below is a trapezoid. Draw a line through the trapezoid that is parallel to the base. Label this line segment *EF* with point *E* being between *A* and *C*.

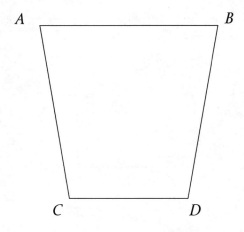

Find the following measures.

$AE =$ _____ $EC =$ _____

$BF =$ _____ $FD =$ _____

Find the following ratios.

$AE/EC =$ _____ $BF/FD =$ _____

What do you notice? _____

_____

_____

What happens when a trapezoid is divided with a parallel line?

_____

_____

Geometry
Set 4: Properties of Lines Cut by Transversals

Station 4

At this station, you will find enough rulers and calculators for all group members. Each person should complete the activity and discuss observations with the group.

In the diagram below, there are two sets of congruent, parallel segments that intersect. Points *a*, *b*, *c*, and *d* are all points at intersections.

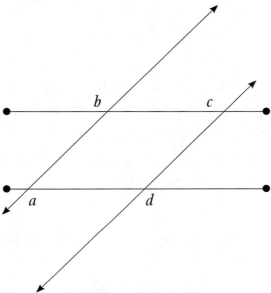

Find the following measures.

$ab =$ _____ $bc =$ _____

$cd =$ _____ $da =$ _____

Find the following ratios.

$ab/cd =$ _____ $bc/da =$ _____

What do you notice? _____

_____

_____

What type of figure is created by intersecting two pairs of parallel segments?

_____

Geometry

Set 5: Properties of Right Triangles

Goal: To provide opportunities for students to develop concepts and skills related to applying properties of right triangles, specifically the Pythagorean theorem

Common Core Standards

Geometry

Understand and apply the Pythagorean theorem.

8.G.6. Explain a proof of the Pythagorean theorem and its converse.

8.G.7. Apply the Pythagorean theorem to determine unknown side lengths in right triangles in real-world and mathematical problems in two and three dimensions.

8.G.8. Apply the Pythagorean theorem to find the distance between two points in a coordinate system.

Student Activities Overview and Answer Key

Station 1

Students will use geoboards to explore right triangles. They need to complete certain tasks and explain the strategies they used to complete those tasks.

Answers: no; answers will vary; answers will vary

Station 2

Students draw their own right triangles and measure the sides. Then they fill out a table to gather information and use that information to draw conclusions about the Pythagorean theorem.

Answers: answers will vary; $a^2 + b^2 = c^2$

Station 3

Students draw their own right triangles and measure the sides. Then they guess what the third side will be and measure to verify their guess. Students explain their strategy for guessing the third side.

Answers: answers will vary; the Pythagorean theorem

Station 4

Students are introduced to Pythagorean triples. They try to find as many as possible using the numbers 1–26. Then they explain their strategy for completing this task.

Number	1	2	3	4	5	6	7	8	9	10	11	12	13
Square	1	4	9	16	25	36	49	64	81	100	121	144	169
Number	14	15	16	17	18	19	20	21	22	23	24	25	26
Square	196	225	256	289	324	361	400	441	484	529	576	625	676

Answers: 3, 4, 5; 6, 8, 10; 5, 12, 13; 9, 12, 15; 8, 15, 17; 12, 16, 20; 15, 20, 25; 7, 24, 25; 10, 24, 26; answers will vary

Materials List/Setup

Station 1   geoboard and rubber bands for each group member

Station 2   calculator, ruler, and protractor for each group member

Station 3   calculator, ruler, and protractor for each group member

Station 4   calculator for each group member

Discussion Guide

To support students in reflecting on the activities and to gather some formative information about student learning, use the following prompts to facilitate a class discussion to "debrief" the station activities.

Prompts/Questions

1. How are geoboards useful when exploring right triangles?

2. When is the Pythagorean theorem useful in real life?

3. If you have a triangle with a hypotenuse of 24 inches and a leg of 9 inches, how long is the other leg?

4. One Pythagorean triple is 3, 4, 5. Another is 6, 8, 10. Is 36, 48, 60 a Pythagorean triple? How do you know?

Think, Pair, Share

Have students jot down their own responses to questions, then discuss with a partner (who was not in their station group), and then discuss as a whole class.

Suggested Appropriate Responses

1. They allow us to make different triangles easily and compare those triangles visually.

2. Many possibilities—when trying to find the distance between two points in a city if you know how many blocks apart they are

3. about 22.25 inches

4. Yes, because 36, 48, and 60 are 12 times the original triple.

Possible Misunderstandings/Mistakes

- Inaccurately measuring sides of a triangle
- Having trouble coming up with Pythagorean triples—guessing rather than having a strategy
- Inaccurately measuring the angles of a triangle

Geometry
Set 5: Properties of Right Triangles

Station 1

At this station, you will find enough geoboards for all group members as well as rubber bands. Each person should complete the activity and then discuss his or her observations and strategies with the group.

Make two different isosceles right triangles on your geoboard. Draw them below.

Do they have the same area? _____

Make two similar right triangles that are not isosceles. Draw them below.

What was your strategy for forming these triangles?

_____

_____

_____

Make a right triangle with an area of three units. Draw it below.

What was your strategy for forming this triangle?

_____

_____

_____

Geometry
Set 5: Properties of Right Triangles

Station 2

At this station, you will find enough protractors, rulers, and calculators for each group member. Each person should complete the activity and discuss his or her observations and strategies with the group.

Draw a right triangle in the space below.

Label the legs a and b, and the hypotenuse c.

Fill in the table below.

Group member	Length a	Length b	Length c	a^2	b^2	c^2	$a^2 + b^2$	$a^2 + c^2$	$b^2 + c^2$

What do you notice? _____

_____

$a^2 + b^2 = $ _____

Geometry
Set 5: Properties of Right Triangles

Station 3

At this station, you will find enough protractors, rulers, and calculators for each group member. Each person should complete the activity and discuss his or her observations and strategies with the group.

Draw a right triangle in the space below.

Label the legs *a* and *b*, and the hypotenuse *c*.

Measure only sides *a* and *b*. Compile your group information in the table below. Fill in only the first three columns.

Group member	Length of *a*	Length of *b*	Guess for *c*	Length of *c*

Work with your group members to guess the length of the hypotenuse. Record this in the table.

Measure the hypotenuse and record this data in the table.

How close were you? _____

_____

What was your strategy for guessing? _____

_____

_____

Geometry
Set 5: Properties of Right Triangles

Station 4

Pythagorean triples are a set of three whole numbers that can be used in the Pythagorean theorem and therefore, could be the sides of a right triangle. An example of this is 12, 35, and 37. $12^2 + 35^2 = 37^2$. Both sides come out to 1369. Now work with your group to find some Pythagorean triples.

Fill in the table below.

Number	1	2	3	4	5	6	7	8	9	10	11	12	13
Square													
Number	14	15	16	17	18	19	20	21	22	23	24	25	26
Square													

Use this information to help you find some Pythagorean triples. Try to name three. (There are nine total using these numbers.)

_____

_____

What was your strategy for coming up with the Pythagorean triples?

_____

_____

_____

_____

Geometry

Set 6: Understanding the Pythagorean Theorem

Goal: To provide opportunities for students to develop concepts and skills related to understanding that the Pythagorean theorem is a statement about areas of squares on the sides of a right triangle

Common Core Standards

Geometry

Understand and apply the Pythagorean theorem.

8.G.6.   Explain a proof of the Pythagorean theorem and its converse.

8.G.7.   Apply the Pythagorean theorem to determine unknown side lengths in right triangles in real-world and mathematical problems in two and three dimensions.

8.G.8.   Apply the Pythagorean theorem to find the distance between two points in a coordinate system.

Student Activities Overview and Answer Key

Station 1

Students draw a triangle and draw the area of each side squared. Then they try to fit the area of the legs squared into the area of the hypotenuse squared. They discuss how this illustrates the Pythagorean theorem.

Answers: Yes; the area of the two legs squared is equal to the area of the hypotenuse squared

Station 2

Students use the Pythagorean theorem to answer a question about the area of land. Then they use the Pythagorean theorem to find distance across a square. This allows students to use the Pythagorean theorem in two different ways for the same problem.

Answers: 5200 square feet; the Pythagorean theorem; about 72 feet

Station 3

Students work though a basic proof of the Pythagorean theorem. They use area to come up with the result.

Answers: c^2; $(1/2)ab$; $2ab$; $c^2 + 2ab$

Station 4

Students determine the area of the squares of two legs of a triangle and compare that to the area of the square of the hypotenuse. Then they explain how this demonstration is related to the Pythagorean theorem.

Answers: 25; 25; they are the same area total; it shows that the two legs squared are equal to the hypotenuse squared

Materials List/Setup

Station 1   pair of scissors, ruler, and pieces of paper for each group member

Station 2   none

Station 3   none

Station 4   none

Discussion Guide

To support students in reflecting on the activities and to gather some formative information about student learning, use the following prompts to facilitate a class discussion to "debrief" the station activities.

Prompts/Questions

1. Why do you use squares to show the Pythagorean theorem in a physical way?

2. What is an example of a real-life situation when you would use the Pythagorean theorem?

3. If the area of a square coming off a leg of a right angle is 64 sq inches and the length of the hypotenuse is 10 sq inches, what is the area of the square coming off the other leg?

4. Explain how you could cut the squares that come off the sides of a right triangle into smaller pieces to find Pythagorean triples.

Think, Pair, Share

Have students jot down their own responses to questions, then discuss with a partner (who was not in their station group), then discuss as a whole class.

Suggested Appropriate Responses

1. In the Pythagorean theorem, the length of the sides are squared which is like finding the area of a square.

2. Many possibilities—finding the distance between two places if you know the horizontal and vertical distance

3. 36 sq inches

4. Example: 3, 4, 5 triangle—cut each square into 4 squares, then you have a 6, 8, 10 triangle

Possible Misunderstandings/Mistakes

- Taking the square root of the amount of land the oldest brother owns
- Having trouble cutting the squares of the legs to fit into the square of the hypotenuse
- Having trouble completing the proof, i.e., not understanding all the steps

Geometry
Set 6: Understanding the Pythagorean Theorem

Station 1

At this station, you will find a pair of scissors, a ruler, and a piece of paper for each group member. Each person should complete the activity and discuss his or her findings with the group.

Draw a right triangle. Now draw squares using each side of the triangle as one side of the squares. There should be three squares. Your figure will look like the one below.

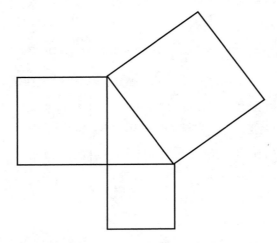

Cut out the squares that are connected to the two legs of the triangle.

See if you can cut them up so they fit inside the square that is connected to the hypotenuse.

Can you? _____

The Pythagorean theorem states that $a^2 + b^2 = c^2$. How does this activity demonstrate that theorem?

_____

_____

_____

_____

Geometry

Set 6: Understanding the Pythagorean Theorem

Station 2

Discuss and answer the following questions as a group.

There are three brothers who own land around a park. The park is in the shape of a right triangle. The park looks like the triangle below. The only land the brothers own is what is directly touching the park (in white).

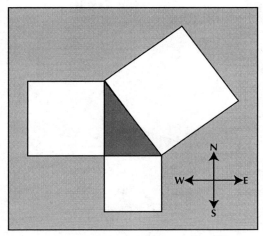

The youngest brother gets the land south of the park. His land is a perfect square, and he has 1600 square feet of land. The middle brother gets the land west of the park. His land is also a perfect square. He has 3600 square feet of land. The oldest brother gets the land that is along the longest section of the park. His land is also a perfect square.

How much land does the oldest brother have? _____

Explain your strategy for solving this problem.

_____

_____

_____

_____

If the oldest brother walked the diagonal across his property, how far would he walk?

_____

Geometry
Set 6: Understanding the Pythagorean Theorem

Station 3

In this activity, you will use a diagram and the area of the diagram to prove the Pythagorean theorem. Look at the diagram below. It is made up of four triangles put together.

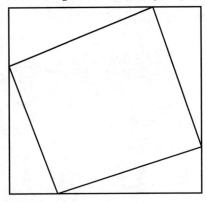

For the purpose of this proof, look at the triangle below.

Now label the sides of the four triangles in the original diagram with *a*, *b*, and *c*. Work together to answer these questions.

What is the area of the small square? _____

What is the area of one of the triangles? _____

What is the area of the four triangles? _____

What is the area of the large square? _____

Geometry
Set 6: Understanding the Pythagorean Theorem

Station 4

At this station, you will explore the Pythagorean theorem and see how it relates to the area of squares. As a group, discuss and answer the questions below.

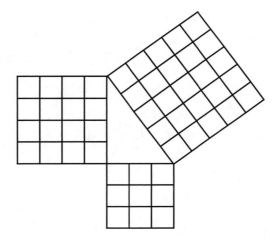

In the figure above, number the boxes in squares that are attached to the two legs of the right triangle (1, 2, 3, etc.).

How many total squares are there? _____

Number the boxes in the square that is attached to the hypotenuse.

How many total squares are there? _____

What do you notice? _____

_____

How does this represent the Pythagorean theorem?

_____

_____

_____

_____

Geometry

Set 7: Volume of Cylinders, Cones, and Spheres

Goal: To provide opportunities for students to practice calculating the volume of cylinders, cones, and spheres

Common Core Standards

Geometry

Solve real-world and mathematical problems involving volume of cylinders, cones, and spheres.

8.G.9. Know the formulas for the volumes of cones, cylinders, and spheres and use them to solve real-world and mathematical problems.

Student Activities Overview and Answer Key

Station 1

Students construct a cylinder out of a sheet of paper. They explore whether the way they choose to roll the paper affects the volume. They experiment and use calculations to answer this question.

Answers: Answers will vary; the cylinder with the 11-inch circumference; 76.9 cubic inches; 63.0 cubic inches; the cylinder with the 11-inch circumference

Station 2

At this station, students use the formula for the volume of a cone ($V = \frac{1}{3}\pi r^2 h$) to determine how many ice cream cones could fit into a cooler. They explain how they do this, and are instructed to be careful with their units.

Answers: πr^2; 4.19 cubic inches; 12 cubic feet; 4,948 cones; you need to change feet to inches or inches to feet so you are working in the same unit, then you can divide the volume of a cone into the volume of the cooler

Station 3

Students determine the volume of several spherical objects by using the formula for the volume of a sphere $\left(V = \frac{4\pi r^3}{3} \right)$. Students measure the circumference of each object using measuring tape, then derive the value of the radius r using the formula for the circumference of a circle ($C = 2\pi r$). They then substitute the value for r into the formula for volume.

Answers: Answers will vary depending on the objects chosen.

Station 4

Students use the formula for the volume of a sphere $\left(V = \dfrac{4\pi r^3}{3} \right)$ to solve problems as a group.

Answers: Answers may vary depending on whether students use a calculator with a π button or if they use the approximate value 3.14 for π. Answers derived using π button:

1. 448π cm^3 or 1407.43 cm^3

2. 576π in^3 or 1809.56in^3

3. $16{,}848\pi$ yd^3 or 52,929.56 yd^3

4. $14{,}580\pi$ mm^3 or 45804.42 mm^3

5. 103.67 cm^3

6. 804.25 mm^3

7. 1357.17 in^3

8. 3015.93 yd^3

9. 3053.63 ft^3

10. 2144.66 mm^3

11. 268.08 cm^3

12. 113.1 yd^3

Materials List/Setup

Station 1   two sheets of paper; tape; mini marshmallows

Station 2   calculator

Station 3   four spherical objects of varying sizes (Ping-Pong balls, orange, basketball, globe, etc.); measuring tape; calculator

Station 4   calculator

Discussion Guide

To support students in reflecting on the activities and to gather some formative information about student learning, use the following prompts to facilitate a class discussion to "debrief" the station activities.

Prompts/Questions

1. Why does the way you roll a rectangle affect the volume of the cylinder you create?

2. Using a real-life example, when is it important to know the volume of an object?

3. What is the formula for the volume of a cylinder?

4. What is the formula for the volume of a cone?

5. What is the formula for the volume of a sphere?

Think, Pair, Share

Have students jot down their own responses to questions, then discuss with a partner (who was not in their station group), and then discuss as a whole class.

Suggested Appropriate Responses

1. If you roll it one way, the length of the rectangle is the height of the cylinder; if you roll it the other way, the length of the rectangle is the circumference of the cylinder.

2. Examples include a can of soup, a storage container, etc.

3. $\pi r^2 h$

4. $(V = \dfrac{1}{3}\pi r^2 h)$

5. $\left(V = \dfrac{4\pi r^3}{3}\right)$

Possible Misunderstandings/Mistakes

- Incorrectly measuring objects
- Incorrectly substituting measurements in the formulas
- Mistaking circumference for radius
- Making arithmetical errors
- Not understanding that the radius is half the diameter of an object

Geometry
Set 7: Volume of Cylinders, Cones, and Spheres

Station 1

At this station, you will find two sheets of paper, tape, and mini marshmallows. Each sheet of paper is 8 ½" × 11". You will be using these to investigate volume.

Your task is to answer this question: Which way should you roll the paper into a cylinder to get the greatest volume? With 11 inches as the circumference or the height? Does it matter?

Tape one sheet of paper into a cylinder so that 11 inches is the circumference. Tape one sheet of paper into a cylinder so that 11 inches is the height.

Which do you think holds more? _____

Fill both cylinders with mini marshmallows.

Which cylinder holds more? _____

Now calculate the volume of the two cylinders. Write your solution below.

Volume of cylinder with 11" circumference: _____
Volume of cylinder with 11" height: _____

Which cylinder has a greater volume? _____

Geometry
Set 7: Volume of Cylinders, Cones, and Spheres

Station 2

At this station, you will pretend you are an ice cream vendor. You have a cooler that is 3 feet × 2 feet × 2 feet. You want to fit in as many ice cream cones as possible. Each ice cream cone is pre-wrapped and has ice cream in it, so you cannot fit them inside one another.

The way to find the volume of a cone is the same as finding the volume of a pyramid: $-\left(\dfrac{1}{3}\right)bh$. In the case of the cone, the base is not found by multiplying the length times the width.

How do we find the area of the base of a cone? _____

_____

_____

Each ice cream cone is 4 inches tall, and the radius is 1 inch.

What is the volume of one ice cream cone? _____

What is the volume of the cooler? _____

How many ice cream cones can you fit in the cooler? (Be careful of your units!)

_____

Explain how you arrived at your solution. _____

_____

_____

_____

Geometry
Set 7: Volume of Cylinders, Cones, and Spheres

Station 3

At this station, you will find a calculator, measuring tape, and several round objects. Work as a group to determine each object's approximate volume by following the steps below.

1. First, use the measuring tape to measure around the middle of each object. This is the circumference (C).

   _____

2. Use this variation of the formula for circumference of a circle to find the radius (r) of the object.

   Radius of a circle: $r = \dfrac{C}{2\pi}$

   _____

3. Finally, substitute the radius into the formula for the volume of a sphere:

   Volume of a sphere: $\left(V = \dfrac{4\pi r^3}{3} \right)$

   _____

4. Use the information to fill in the table.

Object circumference	Radius	Volume

Geometry
Set 7: Volume of Cylinders, Cones, and Spheres

Station 4

Work as a group to solve the following problems. You may use a calculator. Round to the nearest hundredth if necessary.

$$\pi \approx 3.14$$

For problems 1–4, find the volume of a cylinder using the given information.

Volume of a cylinder: $\pi r^2 h$

1. Radius = 8 cm; height = 7 cm

    Volume = _____

2. Radius = 6 in.; height = 16 in.

    Volume = _____

3. Radius = 36 yd; height = 13 yd

    Volume = _____

4. Radius = 18 mm; height = 45 mm

    Volume = _____

continued

Geometry
Set 7: Volume of Cylinders, Cones, and Spheres

For problems 5–8, find the volume of a cone using the given information.

Volume of a cone: $V = \dfrac{1}{3}\pi r^2 h$

5. Radius = 3 cm; height = 11 cm

    Volume = _____

6. Radius = 8 mm; height = 12 mm

    Volume = _____

7. Radius = 9 in.; height = 16 in.

    Volume = _____

8. Radius = 12 yd; height = 20 yd

    Volume = _____

continued

Geometry
Set 7: Volume of Cylinders, Cones, and Spheres

For problems 9–12, find the volume of a sphere using the given information.

$$\text{Volume of a sphere:} \left(V = \frac{4\pi r^3}{3} \right)$$

9. Radius = 9 ft

    Volume = _____

10. Radius = 8 mm

    Volume = _____

11. Radius = 4 cm

    Volume = _____

12. Radius = 3 yd

    Volume = _____

Statistics and Probability

Set 1: Data and Relationships

Goal: To guide students to an understanding of modeling, using linear and quadratic regression to analyze data sets

Common Core Standards

Statistics and Probability

Investigate patterns of association in bivariate data.

8.SP.1. Construct and interpret scatter plots for bivariate measurement data to investigate patterns of association between two quantities. Describe patterns such as clustering, outliers, positive or negative association, linear association, and nonlinear association.

8.SP.2. Know that straight lines are widely used to model relationships between two quantitative variables. For scatter plots that suggest a linear association, informally fit a straight line, and informally assess the model fit by judging the closeness of the data points to the line.

8.SP.4. Understand that patterns of association can also be seen in bivariate categorical data by displaying frequencies and relative frequencies in a two-way table. Construct and interpret a two-way table summarizing data on two categorical variables collected from the same subjects. Use relative frequencies calculated for rows or columns to describe possible association between the two variables.

Student Activities Overview and Answer Key

Station 1

Working with groups, students analyze a data set to find a linear relationship between variables. Students use visual estimates and the median-median line to find the line of best fit.

Answers

1.

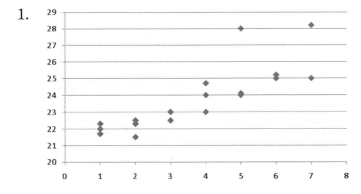

2. yes

3. Answers will vary but should be in the form $y = mx + b$.

4. Answers will vary.

5.

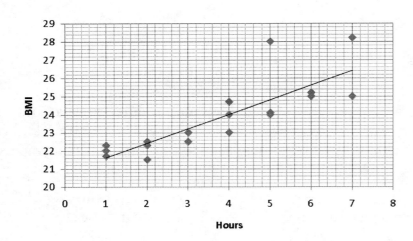

6. No. There are too many other factors involved (such as activity level and diet). There seems to be a correlation, but we can't prove causation.

7. Yes; (5, 28) and (7, 28.2)

Station 2

Working with groups, students analyze a data set to find a linear relationship between variables. Students use a calculator to conduct linear regression.

Answers

1.

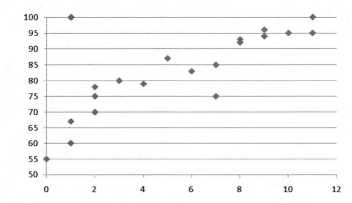

2. yes

3. Answers will vary.

4. (1, 100)

5. $y = 3x + 64$

6. Yes. The linear relationship is very close.

7. We can't prove causation from this data. As the outlier shows, some people may not study because they already know the material well.

Station 3

Students will predict the results of a scatter plot based on information given. They will also examine scatter plots and describe the relationships shown between two data sets.

Answers

1. Answers will vary. Sample answer: The scatter plot might show a positive correlation. Usually students who study more do better. However, it is also possible that the scatter plot shows no correlation. Sometimes students who don't study much do just as well or better than those who study a lot.

2. a positive correlation

3. There appears to be no relationship between the two rankings.

4. a

Station 4

Students will examine scatter plots and make predictions. They will describe the relationship between two sets of data and determine a negative correlation between data sets.

Answers

1a. 35 kPa

1b. 11,000 meters

2a. The scatter plot does not show a relationship. There is no correlation between the two data sets.

2b. No, I would not think there would be any correlation between the number of dollars spent at the mall and the number of e-mails sent.

3. a

4. No, it would not fit the relationship. The scatter plot shows that as you get older, you get taller. A 25-year-old who is 76 cm tall would not show the same relationship.

Materials List/Setup

Station 1	calculator; colored pens or pencils
Station 2	calculator; colored pens or pencils
Station 3	none
Station 4	none

Discussion Guide

To support students in reflecting on the activities and to gather some formative information about student learning, use the following prompts to facilitate a class discussion to "debrief" the station activities.

Prompts/Questions

1. What is a scatter plot?

2. What is regression analysis?

3. What is correlation?

4. What is causation?

Think, Pair, Share

Have students jot down their own responses to questions, then discuss with a partner (who was not in their station group), and then discuss as a whole class.

Suggested Appropriate Responses

1. A scatter plot is a graph of many different sets of variables as points on a grid.

2. Regression analysis means attempting to find a linear or quadratic equation that connects the points in a scatter plot and gives a pattern to the data.

3. Correlation is a relationship between variables.

4. Causation is a relationship in which one variable causes the other one to behave in a certain way.

Possible Misunderstandings/Mistakes

- Incorrectly graphing points

- Incorrectly finding medians

- Confusing medians with means

- Incorrectly using calculator's linear regression and quadratic regression functions

- Confusing correlation with causation

- Incorrectly applying the formula of a line

- Incorrectly applying the formula of a parabola

- Misunderstanding the scenario that provides the data set

Statistics and Probability
Set 1: Data and Relationships

Station 1

Work with your group to answer each question about the data set. Use the calculator to calculate medians, if needed.

A doctor is trying to find out whether there is a correlation between TV viewing and high body mass. She records average daily viewing habits and takes Body Mass Index (BMI) measurements from 18 people.

TV (hours)	BMI	TV (hours)	BMI
1	22	2	22.3
3	22.5	4	23
5	24.1	6	25.2
7	25	2	21.5
4	24.7	5	28
7	28.2	6	25
5	24	2	22.5
1	22.3	1	21.7
3	23	4	24

1. Graph the doctor's results on a scatter plot. Use graph paper.

2. Does there seem to be a linear relationship between the variables?

3. Estimate the equation for the line of best fit.

4. Draw your line in a different color on the scatter plot.

5. Find the equation for the median-median line. Draw it on the scatter plot in a third color.

6. Can you claim with certainty that increased TV viewing causes higher BMI? Explain.

7. Does the graph have any outliers? If so, what are their coordinates?

Statistics and Probability
Set 1: Data and Relationships

Station 2

Work with your group to answer each question about the data set. Use the calculator to calculate medians and create your graphs.

A class wants to find out if there is a correlation between the number of hours studied and grades on the midterm exam. The 20 students log their hours and their grades, as follows.

Studying (hours)	Grade	Studying (hours)	Grade
10	95	2	78
1	60	2	75
7	75	8	92
11	100	3	80
1	100	0	55
2	70	4	79
9	94	9	96
7	85	6	83
5	87	1	67
8	93	11	95

1. Enter the numbers into your calculator to graph the results on a scatter plot. Sketch your plot below.

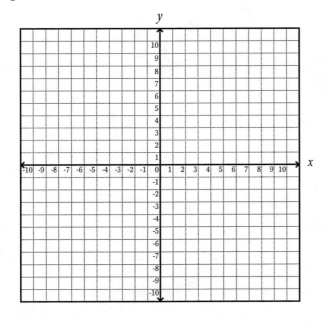

continued

Statistics and Probability
Set 1: Data and Relationships

2. Does there seem to be a linear relationship between the variables?

3. Estimate the equation for the line of best fit.

4. Are there any outliers? If so, what are their coordinates?

5. Use the calculator to find the equation for the line of best fit.

6. Is there a correlation between the variables? Explain.

7. Is there a causative relationship between the variables? Explain.

Statistics and Probability

Set 1: Data and Relationships

Station 3

Work with your group to answer the following questions about scatter plots.

1. Anastasia earns high scores on her vocabulary quizzes because she studies a lot! Anastasia's teacher made a list of the most recent quiz scores of 30 of her students. Then she asked each student how many minutes he or she studied for the quiz. She made a scatter plot with the data. What do you think the scatter plot might have shown? Explain.

2. Examine the scatter plot below. What type of relationship do you see between the two sets of data?

Station Activities for Common Core Mathematics, Grade 8

Statistics and Probability

Set 1: Data and Relationships

3. The scatter plot below shows the relationship between two different rankings for blogs. It shows how a number of blogs were rated in each system. How would you describe the relationship?

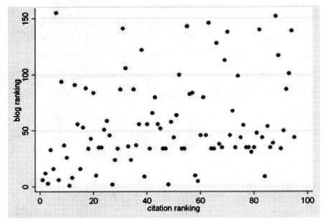

4. Which of the following statements describes the relationship shown in the scatter plot? Circle the letter of the best answer.

a. As the height decreases, the pressure increases.

b. As the height decreases, the pressure decreases.

c. As the height increases, the pressure increases.

Statistics and Probability
Set 1: Data and Relationships

Station 4

Work with your group to answer the following questions about scatter plots.

1. Examine the scatter plot below.

a. What pressure would you expect at a height of 7,500 meters? _____

b. At what height would you expect a pressure of 10 kPa? _____

2. Examine the scatter plot below. The *x*-axis shows the number of dollars each man spent at the mall on Saturday. The *y*-axis shows the number of e-mails each man sent last week.

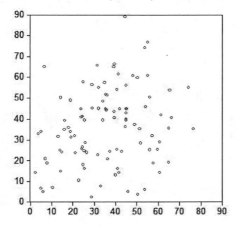

a. What relationship do you see in the scatter plot?

b. Are you surprised by the results of the scatter plot? Explain.

continued

Statistics and Probability

Set 1: Data and Relationships

3. Which scatter plot(s) below show(s) a negative correlation between the two sets of data? Circle the letter(s) of the best answer(s).

a.

c.

b.

d.

4. The scatter plot below shows the age and height of a sample of individuals. If you added a mark for a 25-year-old who is 76 cm tall, would that fit the relationship exhibited in the scatter plot? What relationship does the scatter plot show? Explain.

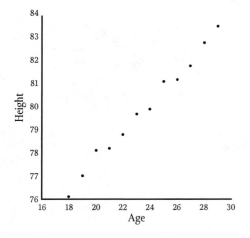

Statistics and Probability

Set 2: Scatter Plots

Goal: To provide opportunities for students to develop concepts and skills related to analyzing data using appropriate graphs

Common Core Standards

Statistics and Probability

Investigate patterns of association in bivariate data.

8.SP.1. Construct and interpret scatter plots for bivariate measurement data to investigate patterns of association between two quantities. Describe patterns such as clustering, outliers, positive or negative association, linear association, and nonlinear association.

8.SP.2. Know that straight lines are widely used to model relationships between two quantitative variables. For scatter plots that suggest a linear association, informally fit a straight line, and informally assess the model fit by judging the closeness of the data points to the line.

8.SP.4. Understand that patterns of association can also be seen in bivariate categorical data by displaying frequencies and relative frequencies in a two-way table. Construct and interpret a two-way table summarizing data on two categorical variables collected from the same subjects. Use relative frequencies calculated for rows or columns to describe possible association between the two variables.

Student Activities Overview and Answer Key

Station 1

Students will work as a group to analyze a scatter plot. They will draw conclusions based on their observations and use those conclusions to make general statements and predictions.

Answers: Number of hours spent studying and test scores; The more a student studies for the test, the higher that student's score; between a 65 and 70; We looked at where one half is on the scatter plot and looked at the other points around that area.

Station 2

Students will work as a group to analyze scatter plots. They will also use a table to make their own scatter plot. They will describe the relationships they see.

Answers

1. It is a positive correlation. The relationship appears to be linear.

2. 65

3. 22

4.

5. There does not appear to be any correlation between the number of hours spent in the mall and the number of dollars spent.

6. There is a positive relationship between height and weight. As one increases, the other increases.

Station 3

Students will make a line graph from a table of data. They will identify the relationship (direct) between the two variables and will come up with some examples of similar relationships.

Answers:

Direct relationship between speed and distance traveled—the faster, the farther. Answers for other examples will vary but should represent direct variation.

Station 4

Students will make a line graph from a table of data. They will identify the relationship (inverse) between the two variables and will come up with some examples of similar relationships.

Answers:

Inverse relationship between education and unemployment—the more education, the lower the unemployment rate. Answers for other examples will vary but should represent inverse variation.

Materials List/Setup

No materials needed.

Discussion Guide

To support students in reflecting on the activities and to gather some formative information about student learning, use the following prompts to facilitate a class discussion to "debrief" the station activities.

Prompts/Questions

1. What conclusions can you draw from a scatter plot if all the points are in a line? What if the points are randomly distributed?

2. What is a good real-life situation to model with a scatter plot?

3. How can a graph help you understand relationships between variables?

4. Describe what you would see in a scatter plot if clustering were present.

Think, Pair, Share

Have students jot down their own responses to questions, then discuss with a partner (who was not in their station group), and then discuss as a whole class.

Suggested Appropriate Responses

1. If the points are in a line, there is a correlation between the two variables. If the points are randomly distributed, one variable does not affect the other.

2. Anything that involves two variables that have a relationship—one affects the other.

3. Plotted points use x and y to represent relationships and line graphs can show a relationship in a set of data points.

4. You would see groups of points plotted in the same area. The points would be grouped together either in one or more groups.

Possible Misunderstandings/Mistakes

- Not understanding how to properly label graphs
- Confusing axes
- Not connecting form of data representation with function
- Misunderstanding relationships between variables

Statistics and Probability
Set 2: Scatter Plots

Station 1

Discuss the following scatter plot with your group, and then work together to answer the questions.

What two pieces of data are being compared in this scatter plot?

What do you notice about the general trend of the data in this scatter plot?

If you were told that a student spent half an hour studying, about what grade would you expect that student to earn on the test?

What information did you use to make that prediction?

Statistics and Probability
Set 2: Scatter Plots

Station 2

Work with your group to examine the scatter plot below and answer questions 1–3.

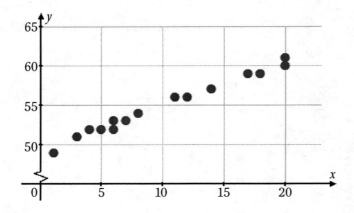

1. Describe the relationship you see between the two sets of data.

2. If you were to guess at the *y*-value that might correspond to an *x*-value of 25, what would you say?

3. If you were to guess at the *x*-value that might correspond to a *y*-value of 63, what would you say?

continued

Statistics and Probability
Set 2: Scatter Plots

The table below shows the number of hours a person spent in the mall and the number of dollars that person spent. Use the table to answer questions 4 and 5.

Hours in mall (x)	Dollars spent (y)
10	40
8	15
9	24
3	20
1	10
2	35
5	50
6	70
7	18
8	25
2	100
3	60

4. Make a scatter plot of the data. Label both axes and title your graph.

continued

Station Activities for Common Core Mathematics, Grade 8

5. Describe the relationship you see in the scatter plot you made on the previous page.

Examine the scatter plot below. Use it to answer question 6.

6. What relationship, if any, do you see between the height and the weight of these 18 statues?

Statistics and Probability
Set 2: Scatter Plots

Station 3

You will be looking at a relationship between two variables and describing other variables that have the same kind of relationship.

The table below contains information about car speed in miles per hour (MPH) and distance traveled in miles. Use it to make a line graph. Label the axes on the lines provided, and give it a title.

MPH	10	20	30	40	50	60	70
Distance traveled in 30 minutes	5	10	15	20	25	30	35

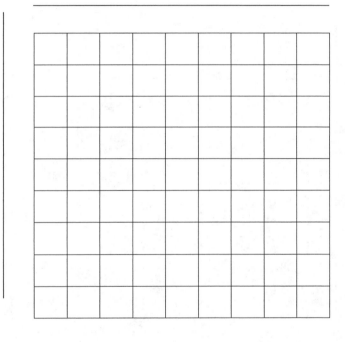

What kind of relationship does the graph show?

What are some other variables that have a similar relationship?

Statistics and Probability
Set 2: Scatter Plots

Station 4

You will be looking at a relationship between two variables and describing other variables that have the same kind of relationship.

The table below contains information about post-high school education and unemployment. Use it to make a line graph. Label the axes of the graph on the lines provided, and give it a title.

Years of education past high school	0	1	2	3	4
Percent of unemployment	9	6	5	4	3

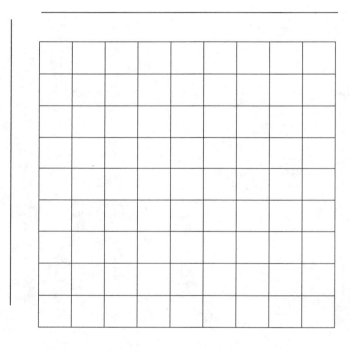

What kind of relationship does the graph show?

What are some other variables that have a similar relationship?